Richbaub's Academy Grammar 1

A Grammar Series for Middle School Writers

by Richard M. Gieson, Jr.

First Edition

© 2018 Richard M. Gieson, Jr.

Richbaub's Ink Works

Support materials for this student workbook, including teacher's answer book and test booklet, are available for download at

www.middleschoolgrammar.com.

Table of Contents

Chapter 1

Getting a Foothold: Prepositions, Nouns, & Pronouns

1.1 – Prepositions & Prepositional Phrases

Prepositions and prepositional phrases are everywhere! Knowing about them will help you immensely when analyzing the parts of a sentence. A good understanding of prepositional phrases will also help advance your writing skills because there are comma and pronoun usage rules associated with prepositional phrases. In addition, advanced writing concepts like agreement, sentence variety, and parallel structure are easier to understand when you know about prepositional phrases. Are you ready? Let's go!

A. **Prepositions** are words that <u>begin little phrases</u> that describe something's or someone's location in space or time (*in* the cupboard, *with* Janie, *above* the house, *after* the movie). These little phrases are called **prepositional phrases**.

B. You will need to memorize a list of prepositions.

C. Here is a list of 40 of the most commonly used prepositions:

about	below	in	out
above	beneath	in front of	over
across	beside	inside	through
after	between	instead of	to
against	beyond	into	toward
along	by	near	under
around	down	next to	until
at	during	of	up
before	for	off	with
behind	from	on	without

D. The best strategies for memorizing the prepositions:

    1. **Break It Up** – Try memorizing in stages by learning 10 (one column) at a time. Once you can recite the first column's prepositions in order, memorize the second column. Then recite both columns in order. Etc.

2. **Learn by Letter Groups** – Work to remember how many prepositions begin with the letter "a." As you can see, there are eight "a" prepositions. Number your paper 1-8 and work on writing down the eight "a" prepositions in order. Once you've mastered the eight "a" prepositions, follow the same strategy for the eight "b" prepositions, the two "d" prepositions, the two "f" prepositions, and so on.

3. **Make Up a Story** – Break your story up into four parts, one for each column of the prepositions above. Try to fill your story with details that are easy to picture in your mind. For example, begin the first column by imagining this scene: <u>About</u> noon <u>above</u> the rocky cliffs <u>across</u> the foamy river, hungry hawks chased <u>after</u> rabbits scurrying below... Memorize one column of your story at a time until you know the whole story. *Not feeling up to creating your own story?* **Check out "Prepositions in Verse" on p. 120 in the appendix of this workbook where you'll find a complete story you can use to help you memorize the prepositions!**

4. **The Airplane Trick** – This technique is not quite as orderly as the others, but it can really help when you get stuck and are trying to remember prepositions you may have forgotten. What you do is picture a bird flying around an airplane—an airplane cruising with its windows open. Now, where can the bird be in relation to the plane? *Inside* the plane, *above* the plane, *behind* it, *in front of* it, *over* it, *under* it, etc. Get it? This technique doesn't work for all of the prepositions in the list above, but you may be able to come up prepositions that aren't on the list that your teacher will be kind enough to give you credit for, like *next to, underneath*, etc. Good luck!

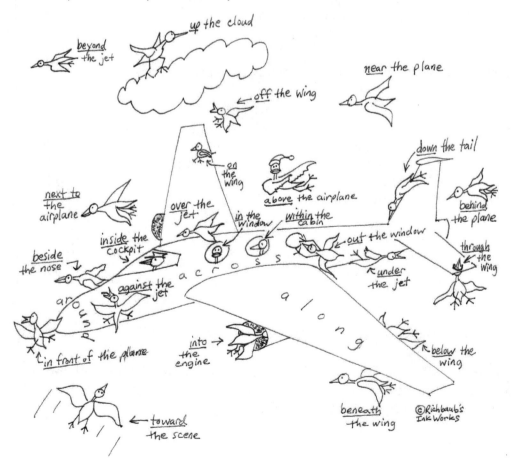

Practice for Evaluation 1

Study the prepositions from the first column on p. 9. When you feel like you're ready, write them below. The first letter of each one has been provided for you.	Now study the prepositions from the second column. When you feel like you're ready, write them below. The first letter of each one has been provided for you.
a_____	b_____
a_____	b_____
a_____	b_____
a_____	b_____
a_____	b_____
a_____	b_____
a_____	d_____
a_____	d_____
b_____	f_____
b_____	f_____

Now study the prepositions from the third column. When you feel like you're ready, write them below. The first letter of each one has been provided for you.	Finally, study the prepositions from the fourth column. When you feel like you're ready, write them below. The first letter of each one has been provided for you.
i_____	o_____
i_____	o_____
i_____	t_____
i_____	t_____
i_____	t_____
n_____	u_____
n_____	u_____
o_____	u_____
o_____	w_____
o_____	w_____

 Evaluation 1: Write a list of 40 prepositions from memory – Are you ready now?

The Basic Structure of a Prepositional Phrase

A. A prepositional phrase begins with a preposition and ends with a noun or pronoun.

B. In between the preposition and the noun or pronoun, there may be one or more descriptive words (adjectives and/or adverbs).

C. Examples:

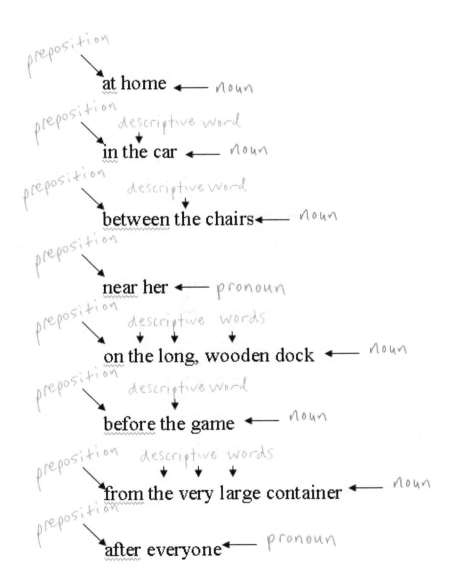

Exercise 1

Write your own prepositional phrases. Use prepositions that begin with the given letters:

1. a _____   4. f _____

2. b _____   5. w _____

3. i _____   6. t _____

SCHOLAR ZONE

Can you imagine a world without writing?

For most of human history there was no writing at all! No books, no magazines, no notes, no letters. Nada, zilch, zero. If only you'd lived 10,000 years ago... Wow, those were the days—NO ESSAY WRITING!! Bummer for you.

English is actually one of the newest written languages.

The first "modern" humans were on earth at least 30,000 years ago. The first time human beings began writing anything down was about 6000 years ago, but the *English* language was born only about 1500 years ago.

Do you know how to make a timeline? If so, try finishing the one below! On the extreme left, mark the approximate beginning of human history. On the extreme right, mark the current year. In between, mark the beginning of writing and the beginning of the English language. Also mark any other historical events you know.

TIMELINE OF WRITING

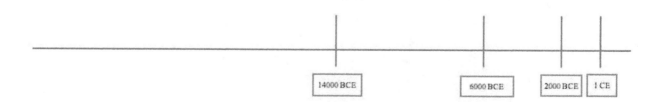

1.2 – Objects of Prepositions

What is an Object of a Preposition and where is it?

A. The last word in a prepositional phrase (the noun or pronoun that completes the phrase) is called the "object of the preposition," or "o.p." for short.

B. In the examples below, the objects of the prepositions are: *home, car, chairs, her, dock, game, container* and *everyone*.

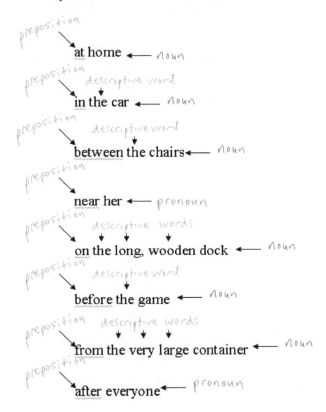

preposition

at home ⟵ noun

preposition   descriptive word

in the car ⟵ noun

preposition   descriptive word

between the chairs ⟵ noun

preposition

near her ⟵ pronoun

preposition   descriptive words

on the long, wooden dock ⟵ noun

preposition   descriptive word

before the game ⟵ noun

preposition   descriptive words

from the very large container ⟵ noun

preposition

after everyone ⟵ pronoun

C. Here are a few more examples of prepositional phrases with their parts labeled inside sentences:

prep.   obj. of prep.   prep.   obj. of prep.

(After the big game) the boys (on the team) ate ice cream sandwiches.

prep.   obj. of prep.

The horse (behind the fence) bit my sister's hand!

D. Sometimes a word from the preposition list appears in a sentence, but it is NOT functioning as a preposition. You can tell because it has no object (o.p.)

Compare the following sentences. Both use the word *before*, which is on your list of prepositions. However, in only one of the sentences is *before* functioning as a preposition.

>   A. I had a cup of water before bedtime.

>   B. Matt had never seen a bridge so high before.

Above, in sentence "B" the word *before* is NOT a preposition—it has no object and is therefore <u>not</u> beginning a prepositional phrase. In sentence "B" *before* is an adverb.

In sentence "A," "before bedtime" is a prepositional phrase, and so *before* <u>is</u> functioning as a preposition.

E. Here's another example:

>   A. Susan went inside after the ballgame.

>   B. The puppy walked inside the doghouse.

In sentence "A," "inside after the ballgame" is NOT a prepositional phrase. "After the ballgame" is a prepositional phrase, and *inside* is all by itself, functioning as an adverb in this sentence.

In sentence "B," "inside the doghouse" IS a prepositional phrase.

F. Remember how a prepositional phrase is built: It begins with a preposition and ends with a noun or pronoun, and it may also have a descriptive word or two between the preposition and o.p.

"Inside the doghouse" fits this pattern, but "inside after the ballgame" does not fit this pattern because the word *after* is not a descriptive word—it begins its own prepositional phrase, "after the ballgame."

Exercise 2

Part 1: Write prepositional phrases and circle the objects of the prepositions (o.p.'s). Use prepositions that begin with the given letters:

1. t _____

2. a _____

3. f _____

Part 2: In each of the following sentences, put parentheses around each prepositional phrase you see and circle the objects of the prepositions. One sentence does not have a prepositional phrase.

4. The boy at the carnival won three huge stuffed animals.

5. Beneath my bed is a dust bunny village.

6. Mary crossed the river near the old bridge.

7. My black cat has never gone outside before.

8. With a grin my dad tore the wrapping from his birthday presents.

9. At midnight the owl always begins his nightly hooting.

10. Paper is recycled at the factory.

On his birthday my dad received a green owl.

Multiple Objects of Prepositions & Coordinating Conjunctions

A. Once in a while, you see a prepositional phrase that has two or three objects. For example:

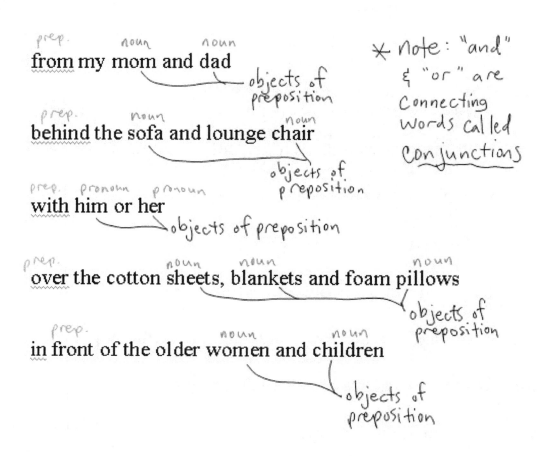

B. When a prepositional phrase has more than one object, we say it has a <u>compound object</u>.

Here are some prepositional phrases with compound objects:

> after the game and picnic
>
> in the drawers and cabinets
>
> with Aubrey, Jermaine, and Michael

Exercise 3

Part 1: Write prepositional phrases that have more than one object of the preposition (o.p.) Use prepositions that begin with the given letters:

1. a _____ *

2. b _____ *

3. u _____

4. w _____

5. i _____

6. o _____

Part 2: In each of the following sentences, put parentheses around the prepositional phrases and circle the o.p.'s. Most of the sentences have more than one prepositional phrase, and some prepositional phrases have compound objects of the preposition.

7. Everybody at the zoo brought money for lunch and souvenirs.

8. Animals on land and sea are hunted by humans.

9. With pencil and paper in hand, I headed to the art room.

10. You can build almost anything with a hammer, nails, and wood.

11. On Monday or Tuesday I will help Tim with his homework.

12. Is your birthday in the summer or in the winter?

13. For tests and quizzes I study with flashcards.

* **See appendix for common mistakes with the prepositions *after*, *before*, and *until*.**

 **Activity**

Make a Prepositional Phrase Poem!

Fall Night	Championship
Inside a circle of rocks	Inside the stadium
On a brisk November evening	Under bright lights
With sticks	In front of the crowd
With marshmallows	On perfect green grass
Under the stars	Among the white lines
Inside our hearts	Between the goals
In my backyard	In colorful uniforms
Into the blackness	With rushing adrenaline
Flicker the bright flames	Swarm the sweating players

What's the pattern? 8-10 prepositional phrases and a final line that looks like this: begins with a verb (an action word), ends with a noun, and includes a descriptive word or two in the middle.

Try it!

Title: _____

1. _____

2. _____

3. _____

4. _____

5. _____

6. _____

7. _____

8. _____

9. _____

10. _____

11. _____

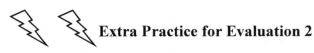 **Extra Practice for Evaluation 2**

Part 1: Surround prepositional phrases with parentheses. One sentence does not have any prepositional phrases.

1. Joe went to the game at the stadium.

2. The boy is running around and screaming.

3. Does anyone care about this TV show?

4. After dinner and the concert Jim and Sue seemed quite exhausted.

5. The dogs and cats bark and meow during the nighttime.

Part 2: Write prepositional phrases that have <u>one</u> object of the preposition, and circle each object. Use prepositions that begin with the given letters:

6. b _____

7. f _____

Part 3: Write prepositional phrases that have <u>more than one</u> object of the preposition (compound o.p.), and circle each object. Use prepositions that begin with the given letters:

8. i _____

9. n _____

Part 4: Write sentences that contain <u>two</u> prepositional phrases, and surround each phrase with parentheses.

10. _____

11. _____

Part 5: Write a sentence that has at least one prepositional phrase which includes <u>two</u> objects of the preposition. <u>Surround each phrase with parentheses</u>.

12. _____

_____

 Evaluation 2: Composing Prepositional Phrases – Are you ready now?

1.3 – Introduction to Nouns & Pronouns

Armed with a sound knowledge of nouns and pronouns, you will be more skilled at telling where a prepositional phrase ends as well as better able to identify subjects in a sentence, which is something coming up in Chapter 5. Advanced writing concepts are also linked to an understanding of nouns and pronouns, things like when to use I *vs. when instead to use* me, *how subject-verb agreement works, and how using concrete nouns can improve the detail and imagery in your writing.*

In addition, all prepositional phrases end with either a noun or a pronoun, so this is an excellent time to review nouns and pronouns.

Noun Basics

A. A **noun** is the most basic part of speech in the universe. Nouns are the words we use for the people, places, things, and ideas all around us, words like *boat, freedom, Africa, fork, grass, pencil,* etc.

B. The nouns that we always capitalize, like the names of people and countries, are called **Proper Nouns**. All other nouns are considered **Common Nouns**.

C. The nouns that describe things you experience with one of your five senses (touch, taste, sight, smell, or hearing) are called **Concrete Nouns**. For example, *paper, car, breeze, aroma, flower,* and *thunder* are all concrete nouns.

D. Nouns that describe things you <u>cannot</u> experience with one of your five senses, things like *liberty, fairness, sin, hope,* etc. are called **Abstract Nouns**.

E. And be sure to recognize that nouns can be proper *and* concrete at the same time, or abstract *and* common at the same time, etc.

Humor Break!

"An abstract noun," the teacher said, "is something you can think of, but you can't touch it. Can you give me an example of one?"

"Sure," a teenage boy replied, "my father's new car."

Exercise 4

Part 1: Using prepositions that begin with the given letters, write prepositional phrases that have…

proper nouns for objects of the preposition (o.p.'s)

1. u _____

2. i _____

3. b _____

concrete nouns for o.p.'s

7. i _____

8. o _____

9. f _____

common nouns for o.p.'s

4. a _____

5. o _____

6. n _____

abstract nouns for o.p.'s

10. w _____

11. d _____

12. t _____

Part 2: Surround prepositional phrases with parentheses. One sentence does not have any prepositional phrases.

13. In Oregon it can be quite rainy along the coast.

14. Everyone from the city and suburbs should vacation in the countryside during the summer months.

15. I have never seen a wild boar outside.

16. Johnson ran over the hill near the grocery store on his way to school.

SCHOLAR ZONE

The English alphabet we use today was influenced by an ancient alphabet called the "Runic" alphabet. The Runic alphabet was invented in the northern regions of Europe long before the English language was born.

Below, under each Runic letter is the letter you know that matches the sound represented by the Runic letter.

Runic   ᚠ ᛒ ᛘ ᛞᛗ ᚠ ᚷ ᚺ ᛁ   ᛚ ᛏ ᛗ ᚾ ᚠ ᚲ   ᚱ ᚢ ᛏ ᚷ   ᚦ ᛦ ᛌ ᚠ ᛉ ᛪ ᛭ ᚦ ᛟ

Modern English   A B C D E F G H I J K L M N O P Q R S T U V W X Y Z

Do you see any similarities between Runic and Modern English letters?

Warning… Super Scholar Zone!

       How come there are no Runic letters for "J" or "V"?

       What do you think those <u>extra</u> Runic letters are for?

Spell out your name using Runic letters. (Use Modern English letters for "J" and "V" if your name includes those letters.):

_____ (Do you like it?)

Pronoun Basics

A. **Pronouns** are a close cousin to nouns. Pronouns are alternate words we use for people, places, things, and ideas. For instance, in place of the nouns *Joe* and *Mary*, you might instead simply use the pronoun *they*. Instead of saying the noun *box*, you could use the pronoun *it*.

B. As you can see, although pronouns are used for the same kinds of things as nouns (people, places, things, and ideas), pronouns are not as specific as nouns.

C. One reason pronouns exist, however, is to provide us some variety.

D. Here's what a world without pronouns might sound like:

> *"Bob and Mabel were married after Bob got out of the Navy. Bob flew Navy jets. Bob was 18 when Bob met Mabel, but Bob didn't have the courage to ask Mabel to marry Bob until Bob turned 25, so Bob and Mabel dated for over seven years before Bob and Mabel got married."*

With pronouns you can refer to someone named Bob as *he* or *him* or someone named Mabel as *she* or *her* once in a while instead of saying their specific names all of the time. Isn't that just wonderful?

Pro-noun Rally

E. Pronouns simplify your life, too.

For example, let's say you were named Jimbo, and you and seven friends went out to a movie. The next day your dad returns from a long business trip, and you and your dad are eating a meal together. In a world without pronouns, the conversation would go something like this:

> **Dad:** *"Ah, good to be back home."*
>
> **Jimbo:** *"Yeah, nice to have Dad back, too, Dad."*
>
> **Dad:** *"So, Jimbo, what has Jimbo been up to?"*
>
> **Jimbo:** *"Last night Bob, Tyler, Nick, Mike, Kevin, Doug, Curly, and Jimbo went to the movies."*
>
> **Dad:** *"Did Jimbo and Jimbo's friends like the movie?"*
>
> **Jimbo:** *"Yeah, Bob, Tyler, Nick, Mike, Kevin, Doug, Curly, and Jimbo loved the movie."*
>
> **Dad:** *"Did Jimbo or Jimbo's friends get any popcorn?"*
>
> **Jimbo:** *"Nah. Neither Jimbo nor Bob, Tyler, Nick, Mike, Kevin, Doug, or Curly had any money left over."*

Instead of naming all of the people you're talking about, you can simply say *everyone*, or *they*, or *we*. Isn't that a nice thing?

Do you see the need for pronouns?

F. The toughest thing to know about pronouns is all the different types of pronouns. We're going to concern ourselves with Personal Pronouns first.

1.4 – Personal Pronoun Usage in Prepositional Phrases

A. **Personal Pronouns** are by far the most-used pronouns, and the most widely *mis*-used, too! There are two main types of personal pronouns. One kind can NEVER be used in a prepositional phrase.

Objective Case Personal Pronouns	Nominative Case Personal Pronouns
me	I
you	you
her	she
it	it
him	he
us	we
them	they
*whom	*who

As you can see, *you* and *it* are both objective and nominative case personal pronouns. They are "all-purpose" personal pronouns.

*Technically, *whom* and *who* are **not** personal pronouns. However, they behave exactly like personal pronouns, and so we are going to consider them to be personal pronouns from here on out! See appendix.

*There is also a **third** case of personal pronouns, the possessive case. See appendix.

B. What's most important here is that when using Personal Pronouns as objects of prepositions, you MUST choose a word on the Objective Case Personal Pronouns list. Get it? OBJECTIVE case for OBJECTS of the preposition?

C. In other words…**The words** *I*, *she*, *he*, *we*, *they*, **and** *who* **can NEVER be used in prepositional phrases!!**

Examples:

CORRECT:	John went fishing (with me and my dad). *"…with my dad and I" would be incorrect*
INCORRECT:	(To my mom and I), chocolate is a wonderful thing. *"To me and my mom" would be correct*
INCORRECT:	They sat (near Bill and I). *"…near me and Bill" would be correct*
CORRECT:	This magazine article is (about him and us). *"…about he and we" would be incorrect*

D. Here are some things to know that can help you remember which personal pronouns are objective case and which ones are nominative case:

Objective Case Pronouns – **O**K for o.p.'s

Most have an "m"

Only *me* ends in "e"

Acronym: Notice that the last letters can spell out "Mr. Tummes."

Nominative Case Pronouns – **N**EVER use for o.p.'s

None contain an "m"

Several end with "e"

Acronym: Arranged as below, the last letters spell out "Tie Eye" followed by a picture of a tie (the "U" in *you*) and a picture of an eye (the "O" in *who*).

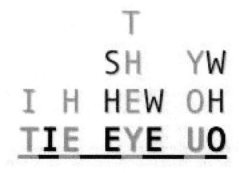

E. Below, fill in the Objective and Nominative Case Personal Pronouns yourself:

Objective Case – **O**K for Prepositional Phrases

Personal
Pronoun
List:

he
her
it
you
them
us
she
they
him
we
whom
who
me
I

M R   T U M M E S
_____

Nominative Case – **N**EVER use in Prepositional Phrases*

T I E   E Y E   U O

* of course, it's ok to use *you* and *it* in prepositional phrases

 **Exercise 5**

You will need to use Personal Pronouns for this exercise:

Personal Pronoun Refresher Box

Objective Case Personal Pronouns	Nominative Case Personal Pronouns
me	I
you	you
her	she
it	it
him	he
us	we
them	they
whom	who

As you can see, *you* and *it* are both objective <u>and</u> nominative case personal pronouns. They are "all-purpose" pronouns!

Part 1: Write prepositional phrases…

that have a personal pronoun for each object of the preposition (o.p.)

1. a _____

2. t _____

3. i _____

where each has <u>two</u> personal pronoun o.p.'s.

4. n _____

5. b _____

6. w _____

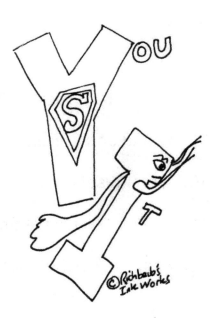

Part 2: Circle only the <u>correct</u> prepositional phrases:

7. between you and I

8. for Jim and me

9. for me and them

10. to me

11. from you and her

12. to who

13. beneath whom

14. with she

15. with her

16. to her and I

Extra Practice for Evaluation 3

Part 1: Write prepositional phrases using a different personal pronoun for each o.p. Also, use prepositions that begin with the given letters.

1. t _____   3. u _____

2. a _____   4. b _____

Part 2: Write prepositional phrases with <u>compound</u> objects. <u>Use only personal pronouns</u> for the objects of the prepositions. Also, use prepositions that begin with the given letters.

5. i _____

6. f _____

7. o _____

Part 3: *Editing for improper prepositional phrase construction.* Put parentheses around each prepositional phrase, and correct any that use personal pronouns incorrectly.

8.   Last weekend there was an intense ping pong match between

9. my dad and I. Before the first game we made a big pitcher of iced

10. tea and set it on a stool next to the table.

11.   "You serve first," said my dad. I smashed a curving serve to

12. him. He flinched but recovered in time and returned it well.

13. "You're getting pretty good with that serve, son," said my dad.

14.   Just then, my twin sisters came into the room. "For who is

15. this tea? Is it for Mary and I?" said my sister Sue.

16.   "No—it's for Dad and me," I shouted between hits.

17.   "Why is he always so mean to us, Dad?" Mary asked.

18.   "He's wrapped up in this game with I," said my dad.

19.   Just then a ball sailed toward her. Mary ducked. The ball

20. ricocheted off the wall and plopped right into the tea pitcher. Sue

21. looked at Mary. Mary looked at Sue. Dad looked at me. "Fine,"

22. I said, "let's give some tea to she and Sue."

23.   "Yuck!" they said. "We don't like ping pong tea!"

 Evaluation 3: Writing Prepositional Phrases + Using Personal Pronouns in Prepositional Phrases – Are you ready now?

BTW: There will be a Personal Pronoun Refresher Box on the test.

SCHOLAR ZONE

Runic	ᚠ ᛒ ᛕ ᛗ ᛘ ᚦ ᚷ ᚻ ᛁ ᛃ ᛐ ᛗ ᚼ ᚠᛚ ᚱ ᚴ ᛏ ᛚ ᚦ ᚤ ᛚ ᛊ ᚠ ᛝ ᛏ ᚼ ᚦ ᚸ
Modern English	A B C D E F G H I J K L M N O P Q R S T U V W X Y Z

So how come writers in England, where English eventually was born, didn't just adopt this weird Runic alphabet that had been hanging around their region and use it when English began to develop? Why does English use the "Modern English" letters above?? Stay tuned—we've only just begun!

P.S. Did you ever make up your own, original alphabet with unique letters? (Why not?) Give it a try and send a friend a secret note!

Your alphabet:

1.5 – Indefinite, Demonstrative, & Reflexive Pronouns

A. **Indefinite Pronouns** – They're called *indefinite* because it's not definite who, what, or how many things you're talking about when you use them.

Agreement, a topic you'll study when you're older, involves rules with indefinite pronouns…

B. *Everyone*, *nothing*, and *somebody* are all indefinite pronouns. In fact, <u>all the words ending in *one*, *thing*, and *body* are indefinite pronouns</u>.

C. Other indefinite pronouns include:

few	neither	many	none
several	any	some	much
both	all	most	one
either	other	more	no one

D. For your information, indefinite pronouns can sometimes switch to being adjectives (a kind of descriptive word):

In the following sentence, *some* is the object of a preposition and a pronoun:

$($To <u>some,</u>$)$ boxing is a barbaric sport.

This next sentence also includes *some*, but it describes the word *people* and is therefore a descriptive word (adjective) and not a pronoun.

Boxing is the greatest sport in the world $($to <u>some</u> people.$)$

In the following sentence, *all* is the object of a preposition and a pronoun:

The Constitution promises life, liberty and the pursuit of happiness $($for <u>all</u>.$)$

Below, *all* describes the word *insects* and is therefore a descriptive word (adjective), not a pronoun.

My mom is terribly frightened $($by <u>all</u> insects.$)$

☆   Do you see how <u>the part of speech of a word depends on how it is used</u>?   ☆

E. **Demonstrative Pronouns** – The pronouns used when you point to something: *this, that, these,* and *those.* These words can also be adjectives, depending on how they're used.

English teachers don't like it when you use demonstrative pronouns in essay conclusions… "That is why…" "This is why…" "Those are the reasons…" Aargh!

For example:

In the following sentence, *these* is the object of a preposition—it's not a descriptive word; it's a pronoun being used in place of the names of all of the things being referred to:

I want you to make room (for <u>these</u>.)

In the sentence below, *these* describes something, so it's functioning as an adjective:

Yesterday I ate a box (of <u>these</u> cookies) for dessert.

F. **Reflexive Pronouns** – Words ending in "self" and "selves" are reflexive pronouns: *myself, yourself, himself, ourselves, themselves,* etc.

A reflexive pronoun reflects on his reflection.
©Richbaub's Ink Works

Words like "hisself," "theirselves," "themself," etc. are NOT real words!

Exercise 6

Part 1: Using prepositions that begin with the letters provided, write prepositional phrases that have…

indefinite pronouns for o.p.'s (be sure they're not being used as adjectives!)

1. a _____

2. t _____

3. u _____

reflexive pronouns for o.p.'s

4. i _____

5. w _____

6. b _____

demonstrative pronouns **for o.p.'s**

7. a _____

8. f _____

9. n _____

personal pronouns for o.p.'s

10. o _____

11. b _____

12. i _____

> After you complete this exercise, sketch a picture or make a cartoon that relates to something you've written on this page: (This is an optional activity!)

> Have you noticed yet that the personal pronoun *her* can sometimes act as an adjective? If you use *her*, put it at the end of your prepositional phrase to make sure it is a pronoun.

Part 2: Write sentences of at least ten words that include…

13. A reflexive pronoun:

_____

14. A demonstrative pronoun (be sure your pronoun is not being used as an adjective!):

_____

15. An indefinite pronoun (be sure your pronoun is not being used as adjective!):

_____

Extra Practice for Evaluation 4

Part 1: Using a different preposition for each, write prepositional phrases that have <u>compound</u> o.p.'s.

use demonstrative pronouns for both o.p.'s: use indefinite pronouns for both o.p.'s:

1. _____   3. _____

use personal pronouns for both o.p.'s: use a reflexive pronoun for <u>one</u> of the o.p.'s:

2. _____   4. _____

Part 2: Write one prepositional phrase where the word *that* is used as an o.p. and one prepositional phrase where the word *that* is a descriptive word (adjective).

that as an o.p.:   *that* as a descriptive word (adjective):

5. _____   6. _____

Part 3: Recalling the pronoun types.

7. Write out the personal pronouns you are allowed to use in prepositional phrases (hint – Mr. Tummes):	8. Write eight indefinite pronouns:
9. Write five reflexive pronouns:	10. Write out the four demonstrative pronouns:

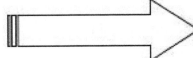

Part 4: Put parentheses around each prepositional phrase, and correct any prepositional phrases where personal pronouns are used incorrectly.

11. In a quiet backyard in the town of Chester, three boys played a

12. game of kickball. Mike was up first. "Roll a nice, slow one to me," he

13. called out to the pitcher.

14. "If you kick one to Dennis or I, you're a dead duck!" said Richie,

15. who was pitching. Richie turned and whispered to Dennis, "Move over

16. to the left. We'll nail him if he goes for second base." Dennis was

17. moving over when, at that moment, Mike stroked a ball between Richie

18. and he. Dennis chased it to the fence. "Throw it to me!" yelled Richie.

19. Mike rounded first base and wondered to himself if he could

20. beat Dennis's throw to second base. Mike's eyes widened as Dennis

21. released a laser through the hot summer air toward him, Richie, and

22. second base, but it was rising and the ball whizzed completely over the

23. heads of Richie and he. Mike raced for third base.

24. "If Richie and I lose," thought Dennis, "I'll be really upset with

25. myself." Racing for the loose ball, Richie grabbed it, whirled, and,

26. falling away, whipped it at Mike. Thwack!

27. "I'll get you for this, Richie," said Mike as he examined the welt

28. developing on his leg, for his furious race around the bases had

29. suddenly ended just inches from home plate!

 Evaluation 4: Using Pronouns in Prepositional Phrases – Are you ready now?

BTW: There will be a Personal Pronoun Refresher Box on the test.

1.6 – Comma Usage with Introductory Prepositional Phrases

A. When beginning a sentence with one or more prepositional phrases, people often have an urge to use a comma afterward. However, there is no strict grammar rule about this.

Using commas after introductory prepositional phrases (prep. phrases at the beginning of sentences) is actually <u>optional</u>.

"I hate commas in the wrong places."
- *Walt Whitman, famous American poet*

B. Good writers know, though, that using commas unnecessarily is bad form. So, **after one introductory prepositional phrase, you should mostly <u>avoid</u> using a comma:**

Compare the following sentences:

    At school I look forward to recess the most.

    At school, I look forward to recess the most.

The comma in the second sentence above is <u>not</u> necessary and should therefore be omitted.

C. **Once in a while, you need to use a comma after a single introductory prepositional phrase in order to avoid confusion.**

Compare the following sentences:

    To some French dressing on a salad adds zest to any meal.

    To some, French dressing on a salad adds zest to any meal.

The comma definitely helps—without the pause you might think the sentence is about either how only some French people like dressing on their salads or even how some French folks enjoy getting dressed on top of a salad!

D. Also, there are certain prepositional phrases typically used at the beginning of a sentence that REALLY make you feel like inserting a comma after them. **After phrases like "for example," "in other words," "in conclusion," "by the way," etc., it's ok to use a comma.**

E. After <u>more than one</u> introductory prepositional phrase, commas are more acceptable but still optional:

Compare the following sentences:

> In the corner of my bedroom I saw a large roach climbing the wall.

> In the corner of my bedroom, I saw a large roach climbing the wall.

The comma in the second sentence is acceptable since there are two prepositional phrases beginning the sentence, but is it really necessary?

F. The bottom line? **After prepositional phrases at the beginning of sentences, if you can do without a comma, don't use one.**

Never throw commas around whenever and wherever you want for no good reason. A "gut feeling" is not a good enough reason!

(Other comma rules are stricter, like those regarding compound sentences or items in a series, etc. Do you know some of these commas rules?)

Ultimately, good writers use a comma <u>only when their gut feeling lines up with a grammatical rule</u>; otherwise, commas are to be avoided.

Extra Practice for Evaluation 5

Part 1: Write sentences of 8-12 words that begin with one or two prepositional phrases. Pay close attention to comma usage. Surround each prepositional phrase with parentheses.

1. _____

_____

2. _____

_____

3. _____

_____

4. _____

_____

Part 2: Locating Prepositional Phrases in sentences and identifying Objects of Prepositions

Surround each prepositional phrase with parentheses, and circle each object of the preposition.	Is the o.p. a noun (N) or a pronoun (PRO)?
5. The meal provided enough food for everyone.	
6. Two eagles were soaring high in the sky above.	
7. The clothes on display were very colorful.	
8. The squirrel scurried up the giant redwood tree.	
9. A tornado circled the town just after midnight.	
10. For many, Irish stew is a hearty meal.	

 Evaluation 5: Nouns vs. Pronouns + Comma Usage with Introductory Prepositional Phrases – Are you ready now?

Chapter 2

Punctuating Dialogue

2.1 – Introduction to Punctuating Dialogue

Have you read any books lately? Well, if you have, and I assume that you have, then you know that dialogue is
ALL OVER THE PLACE!

The funny (scary?) thing is, however, that even though you constantly see dialogue in the books you read, you STILL
don't realize that two people can NEVER speak in the same paragraph, that there is ALWAYS punctuation at the
end of a quotation, or that words like "said" are NEVER capitalized.

Seriously, you need to pay attention to the info in this chapter!

A. "Dialogue" means that two or more people are speaking to each other. Writers often record what other people say, so it's important to know how to correctly punctuate dialogue in your writing.

B. Even when you're recording what just one person said or is saying, you need to punctuate it in a certain way.

C. Quotation marks are only part of the punctuation you will need when quoting someone. You also need commas and periods in just the right places. Paying attention to capital and lower-case letters is also important.

Tired of being in all the wrong places, some brave punctuation decides to make a change.

JUST the RIGHT PLACE!

Let's go!

©Richbaub's Ink Works

2.2 – Quotation Marks in Dialogue

A. Quotation marks (" ") are used at the beginning and end of a quotation. They surround what someone says:

Examples:

    1. "Fish swim," said Joe.

    2. Joe said, "I like white bread. I also like flour tortillas."

B. Notice that quotation marks do not go around each sentence someone says. They start when someone begins to speak, and they're not used again until he or she is finished speaking.

C. Sometimes single quotation marks are used. Single quotation marks, however, are only used with a quotation inside of another quotation.

Example:

    William said, "I love it when the baby says, 'Goo goo.' It really makes me laugh!"

D. **Quick Practice** – Add quotation marks to the following dialogue:

Mom said , Will you be home early tonight ?

Dad said , I don't think so . I've got to finish a project .

I said , You work too much , Dad . We miss you !

But this morning you said , I'll take you guys to a movie tonight , said my brother .

Dad said , I'm sorry . I'll make it up to you this weekend .

2.3 – Commas & End Marks in Dialogue

A. Look at the <u>end marks</u> (periods, exclamation points, and question marks) and <u>commas</u> in the following exchange between Robert and Teresa:

"You told me I could buy this candy bar for one dollar," said Robert.

Teresa replied, "That's not what I said. I said it costs two dollars!"

"Really?" said Robert.

"Yes, really!" said Teresa.

B. At the end of every quotation there is some sort of punctuation, and this punctuation is always placed <u>inside</u> the quotation marks, whether it's a comma, period, exclamation point, or question mark.

C. In the second line of dialogue above, there is a comma before the quotation because it's introduced by "Teresa replied." Always use a comma when introducing a quotation with something like "Bob said" or "Joe asked," etc.

D. **Quick Practice** – Add commas and end marks to the following dialogue:

Max said " Do you like peanut butter "

" No, I do not like peanut butter " answered Ann

" Then I guess we can't be friends " said Max

Surprised, Ann said " Wow. You must really love peanut

butter "

2.4 – Capital & Lowercase Letters in Dialogue

A. When beginning a quotation, always capitalize the first letter of the first word of the quotation—even if the quotation begins in the middle of a sentence.

Examples:

"Fish swim," said Joe.

Joe said, "Fish swim."

B. Words like *said, asked, exclaimed, stated,* etc. are **never** capitalized in dialogue—<u>even when they come after an exclamation point or question mark</u>.

Examples:

"We rock!" **e**xclaimed Joe.

"Do bugs sleep?" **a**sked Alex.

"Rain is coming," **s**aid the weatherman.

C. Quick practice – Fill in the missing letters. Pay attention to whether they should be capitalized or not.

Joe __aid, "__hy don't you come over to my house today?"

"__o, I can't," _aid Kent.

"__hy not?" __aid Joe.

Kent replied, "__ecause my mom said I have to do homework!"

2.5 – Interrupted Quotations

A. Sometimes authors don't begin or end a quotation by identifying the speaker. Sometimes authors make a <u>break in the quotation</u> to let the reader know who's speaking.

Compare the following:

1. Joe said, "Pie is good, but cake is totally awesome!"

2. "Lemons are yellow. Bananas are yellow, too," said Joe.

3. "Pie is good," said Joe, "but cake is totally awesome!"

4. "Lemons are yellow," said Joe. "Bananas are yellow, too."

Above, lines 3 and 4 feature interrupted quotations because "said Joe" comes right in the middle of Joe speaking—not before or after he speaks as in examples 1 and 2.

B. With interrupted quotations the punctuation and capitalization are a little bit tricky. For instance, examples 3 and 4 above <u>look</u> very similar, but after "said Joe" the punctuation and capital letter usage is different. Here are the examples again:

3. "Pie is good," said Joe, "but cake is totally awesome."

4. "Lemons are yellow," said Joe. "Bananas are yellow, too."

Why is the punctuation and capital letter usage different where the arrows point?

C. In example 3, "said Joe" is <u>completely interrupting a sentence</u>—and so when you pick the sentence back up after "said Joe" with the word *but*, you go with a comma and a <u>lower-case</u> letter.

D. In example 4, "said Joe" is actually **between** <u>two separate sentences</u>. In this case, you put a **period** after "said Joe" to conclude the first sentence. After "said Joe" a new sentence begins with the word *bananas*, so you go with a **capital letter** as Joe continues to speak.

E. **Quick Practice** - Fill in the missing letters (L) and punctuation (P). Pay attention to whether letters should be capitalized or not.

"__et's meet after school__" __aid Tim__ "__o we can work on the project."
  L   P L   P L

"I can't__" __aid Tonya __ "__y mom can't drive me then."
      P   L   P   L

Tim __aid__ "__y mom can pick you up."
     L   P   L

"__reat__" __aid Tonya __ "__re you sure that's ok?"
 L   P   L   P   L

"No problem!" __aid Tim.
             L

Humor Break!

A zookeeper wanted to get some extra animals for his zoo, so he decided to compose a letter. The only problem was that he didn't know the plural of "mongoose."

He started the letter: "To whom it may concern, I need two mongeese."

No, that won't work. He tried again: "To whom it may concern, I need two mongooses." Is that right?

Finally, he got an idea: "To whom it may concern, I need a mongoose, and while you're at it, send me another one."

2.6 – Multiple Speakers & Paragraph Breaks

A. When you record a conversation, change to a new paragraph when you switch to a different speaker:

> "Let's go to the beach today," said Marcus. "It's too hot to play in the neighborhood."
>
> "Great idea, Marcus," said Louis. "We should call David. He's a great surfer, and I'm sure he would love to come with us." Louis grabbed his cell phone and began dialing David's number.
>
> "Wait!" said Marcus. "I just remembered that David is away on vacation. Let's call Tracey and Meredith instead." Marcus paused. Louis had a funny look on his face, almost like he was suddenly scared of something.
>
> After gulping, Louis finally began to speak. "Tracey and Meredith? Aren't those the girls who just moved here from Hawaii? You know," Louis continued, "they might be better surfers than we are!"
>
> With a sly smile Marcus said, "Scared of a little competition, Lou?"

B. Notice in the dialogue above that you don't always begin or end dialogue paragraphs with quotations. Paragraphs of dialogue can contain a combination of quotation and narration—but no single paragraph should include quotations from two different speakers!

C. The forced paragraph breaks come in handy, too, for with long conversations authors can drop the "he saids" and "she saids" since the paragraph breaks signal that the speaker has changed.

Chapter 2 Review

 Exercise 7

<u>Directions</u>: The following chart contains quotations from a dialogue involving Kevin, James, and their mom.

On the following page, re-write everything in paragraph form using the rules we've discussed about punctuating dialogue.

Not only will you add punctuation and paragraph breaks, but you will also add "Kevin said" and "said James," etc. each time someone speaks. <u>Where you put the "James said" and "said Kevin" can vary, so mix it up a little!</u>

<u>Begin the dialogue with Kevin</u>, and then alternate between the speakers in a way that makes the most sense.

What Kevin said	What James said	What Mom said
Mom says we have to clean up our room before we can go to the game tonight. That's not true. You haven't made your bed for two weeks! Are you blind? Your homework desk is covered with Doritos crumbs! Crud nuggets!	It's mostly your mess. At least I put my clothes away. You, on the other hand, just leave your old clothes wherever you happen to be standing when you undress. You're a total slob, dude! Oh no!	Boys? Jamie just called, and she'll be here to pick you up for the game in five minutes. How does your room look?

Write the dialogue out on the next page.

$\longrightarrow$

Re-write the dialogue here (Begin with Kevin):

_____

_____

_____

_____

_____

_____

_____

_____

_____

_____

_____

_____

_____

Directions: Read through the following dialogue and put a check next to the lines that have NO errors. For lines with errors, leave the line blank, but do correct the mistake(s).

1. _____	One summer day a trout approached a young boy sitting
2. _____	on a dock. "Hey, little boy," said the trout, "The bait you're
3. _____	using is quite delicious. My friends and family are having a
4. _____	hard time avoiding your sharp hook."
5. _____	Startled for a moment, the boy slowly replied "Really?
6. _____	Then how come I haven't caught any of you?"
7. _____	"We are much more clever than you think, little boy" said
8. _____	the trout, "Your hook does from time to time injure us, though.
9. _____	"My little son Jimmy was pricked just a moment ago as he
10. _____	nibbled on your bait."
11. _____	"I knew I'd felt a bite!" Said the little boy.
12. _____	"Indeed. Which brings me to the purpose of this little
13. _____	visit", said the trout.
14. _____	The little boy frowned and said, "Yes, why exactly are
15. _____	you talking to me anyway?" The trout became a bit frightened
16. _____	by the little boy's stern face and glanced away toward the
17. _____	surface of the lake where his family and friends were looking up
18. _____	at him. He regained his courage.
19. _____	"It's just that, well, we're still hungry, and your hook is
20. _____	now empty," said the trout. "could you please put some more
21. _____	bait on for us? We would much appreciate it"!

 Evaluation 6: Punctuating Dialogue – Are you ready?

Chapter 3

The Heart of Good Writing: All About Verbs

3.1 – Introduction to Verbs

Many times, the key to improving a sentence lies in improving the sentence's verb. A better verb can improve a sentence's clarity as well as its imagery, and paying attention to the placement of verbs plays a role in having better sentence variety.

Therefore, a grammatical understanding of verbs is a very powerful thing to possess—it's one of the advantages expert writers have over average writers. Experts' verb knowledge includes knowing the difference between action and linking verbs, understanding helping verbs, and being able to discern the difference between active and passive voice writing. If you pay close attention, you too can possess this special knowledge!

A. In dealing with verbs, it's impossible to avoid mentioning subjects, too.

Do you know what a subject is? A subject is simply the main person or thing a sentence is about. Subjects are always nouns or pronouns.

However, before getting in depth about subjects, it's important to first get in depth about verbs.

B. Every sentence has at least one verb. There are two kinds of verbs: action verbs and linking verbs.

C. Action Verbs

Sometimes the verb tells what the subject of a sentence does, did, or will be doing. This is when the verb is showing <u>action</u>. Verbs showing action have been cleverly named Action Verbs.

> **In the afternoon Bill *built* a bookcase for his son.** (The subject *Bill* did something—he *built* a bookcase.)

D. Action verbs don't just show physical action like *building*, *running*, and *shoving*. They also show mental or emotional activity. The following sentences all have **action verbs**:

1. Jim <u>loves</u> his dog.
2. Susan <u>thought</u> about her project for two weeks.
3. For his birthday my brother <u>wanted</u> a new bicycle.

E. Linking Verbs

Sometimes, a subject of a sentence isn't really doing anything; instead, it is just <u>being</u> something. In this case, the verb is called a Linking Verb because it is the word that <u>links</u> the subject to something the subject is or is being.

> **After the game I <u>was</u> very happy.** (*I* is the subject and *happy* is what the subject was being—these words are linked by the verb *was*.)

> **That notebook <u>is</u> really thick.** (*Notebook* is the subject and *thick* is what it is—these words are linked by the verb *is*.)

F. Compare Action and Linking verbs with the examples below:

Action Verb:

> **Timothy <u>brought</u> the cake to the party.** (*Brought* is a verb showing action—the subject, Timothy, is actually doing something.)

Linking Verb:

> **Timothy <u>was</u> upset yesterday.** (*Was* is a linking verb—the subject, Timothy, is not doing anything; there is no action. Timothy is just <u>being</u> *upset*.)

G. One of the most important things someone can learn regarding grammar is how to tell the difference between action verbs and linking verbs. More on that later.

H. For now, let's concern ourselves with trying to recognize which word in a sentence is the verb.

SCHOLAR ZONE

During the time of the Roman Empire and before the birth of the English language, Romans came to England, or "Britain" as they called it. With them, the Romans brought the alphabet of their Latin language.

Here's the alphabet the Romans brought to England in the first century AD:

Roman Latin   A B C D E F G H I L M N O P Q R S T V X Y Z

The Roman Latin alphabet has fewer letters than our modern English alphabet. **What are the missing letters and sounds?**

Exercise 8: Put a box around action verbs, and mark linking verbs with an "L" shape.

Examples:

a. The boy swung at the fastball.

b. My shoes were in the closet.

1. Under the rock three worms wriggled in the dirt.

2. Toward the end of the vacation we were extremely sad.

3. She knew the answer to every math problem on the test.

4. The football team ran onto the field.

Hint: Verbs are NEVER inside prepositional phrases, so if you first mark prep. phrases, your search for verbs will be easier!

SCHOLAR ZONE

Roman Latin   A B C D E F G H I L M N O P Q R S T V X Y Z

Although the Roman alphabet looks mighty familiar, the Romans themselves did *not* use it for English! The Romans spoke Latin, and this is the alphabet they used to write Latin. (BTW, the word "Latin" comes from the original name of the region in Italy where Rome was built, "Latium.")

Lots of Latin has worked its way into English over the centuries. For instance, you might recognize the following Latin words:

EXIT (to go out)   ABDOMEN (belly)   ALIBI (elsewhere)

Warning… Super Scholar Zone!:

Do you know the meanings of the following Latin words?

TERRA =

ULTRA =

3.2 – Verbs in the Infinitive Form

A. When verbs are first "born," they are in a form called the "infinitive form." The infinitive form of a verb looks a lot like a prepositional phrase—but it's NOT a prepositional phrase!

B. Here's a verb in the infinitive form: **to cook**. Here's another: **to sing**. So the infinitive form is *to* plus a verb.

C. Of course, *to* can also be a preposition, but *to* plus a <u>verb</u> is NOT a prepositional phrase—there are no verbs in prepositional phrases.

D. Below, circle only the <u>prepositional phrases</u>:

to me	to eat	to be	to wonder
to walk	to the store	to Joseph	to begin

Do you understand the difference between infinitives and prepositional phrases beginning with *to*?

E. With a verb in its infinitive form, you can't make a sentence by just adding a subject, i.e. you can't say "Mary to cook." Of course, you can say "Mary cooks." You see, the verbs that have subjects—the ones you need to make a sentence—are never in the infinitive form.

F. Think of an infinitive as an egg. To use the verb, you crack it open and get something completely new and usable.

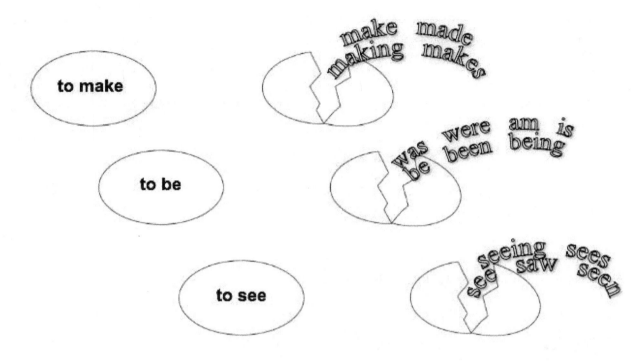

G. You <u>can</u> use verbs in the infinitive form in your sentences. Just remember that an infinitive is never **THE** verb—the one that goes with the subject. In other words, a verb in the infinitive form is never the thing the subject is being or doing.

Examples:

I | like | to go (to the movies) (on Saturdays.)

Above, *I* is the subject and *like* is the verb. "To go" is an infinitive. You see, the subject isn't <u>going</u> anywhere; the subject <u>likes</u> something.

Josephine always | wanted | to be (in a movie) (with a Hollywood star.)

Above, *Josephine* is the subject and *wanted* is the verb. "To be" is an infinitive. Josephine was not <u>being</u> anything; she <u>wanted</u> something.

3.3 – More Verb Forms

A. Verbs have many different forms. The infinitive form is just one form. Two other forms are the present tense and the past tense.

Here is an example of one verb's various forms:

infinitive	present tense		past tense	
to ask	base form	**ask:** "I ask," "We ask," etc.	"ed" form	**asked:** "I asked," "You asked," etc.
	"s" form	**asks:** "She asks," "He asks," etc.		
	"ing" form	**asking:** "I am asking," etc.		

FAQ's:

B. What's the word *am* doing in there right above the arrow??

The word *am* is <u>helping</u> the verb work in this sentence. You couldn't say "I asking."

Actually, *am* has even become part of the verb. The verb in this sentence would be "am asking."

Other words we use to help verbs work are *was, be, were, can, may,* and many more! For example:

<u>was</u> asked   <u>were</u> asking   <u>can</u> ask   <u>may be</u> asking

C. What about the future tense??

To speak about doing something in the future, English requires you to use one or more <u>helping verbs</u>. For example:

She <u>will</u> **ask** you about your homework. *(The verb in this sentence is "will ask.")*

My brother <u>will be</u> **asking** you for a ride to school. *(The verb in this sentence is "will be asking.")*

3.4 – Helping & Main Verbs, a.k.a. Verb Phrases

A. As we just saw, verbs are not always single words (or in the infinitive form). Sometimes a verb is made up of a few words in order to get the verb into just the right tense or to express just the right meaning:

Jenna <u>jogs</u> in the park. (the verb is a single word)

Jenna <u>is jogging</u> in the park. (the verb is made up of two words)

Jenna <u>should have been jogging</u> in the park. (the verb is made up of four words!)

B. Multiple-word verbs are called "verb phrases," so a sentence may contain a single-word verb **OR** a verb phrase.

C. In a verb phrase the last word is the "main verb." The other words are "helping verbs."

Under the bridge Johnny <u>may be fishing</u> for trout.

verb = may be fishing
helping verbs = may, be
main verb = fishing

D. Again, in a verb phrase the last word is always the "main verb;" the other words are "helping verbs." **The whole thing together is what you would call "the verb."** So, if you're looking at a sentence that has a verb phrase and your teacher asks you, "What's the verb in this sentence?", don't just state the <u>main</u> verb—state <u>the entire verb phrase</u>.

E. Words ALWAYS used as <u>just</u> helping verbs:

will would	can could	should	may might must

Factoid

These words weren't always confined to just these forms; their other forms have more or less simply fallen out of usage. English is an ever-evolving language!

"Retired" forms of...

will: wilt, wouldst

could: canst, couldst

should: shall, shalt, shouldst

may: mayest, mayst

F. Words used not only as helping verbs but also as main verbs—and some even as single-word verbs. You might think of these guys as "all-purpose" verbs: *

be	are	is	have	do
been	am	was	had	does
		were	has	did

G. Examples:

He is in the kitchen. (*Is* is single-word verb in this sentence.)

He is swimming in the ocean. (Here, *is* is now a helping verb. *Swimming* is the main verb. What we would call "the verb" is "is swimming.")

I have been to Maine in the summertime. (*Been* is often a helping verb, but in this sentence it is the main verb of a verb phrase. *Have* is a helping verb.)

H. Consider the following sentence:

The team with the star quarterback should have won that game.

Now, if your teacher were to ask you, "What is the verb in this sentence?" of

course you would answer _____ .

Did you answer correctly?

*The *-ing* form of the verb *be* (*being*) also qualifies for this list but is omitted for the sake of simplicity. See appendix for a discussion of <u>participles, infinitives, and gerunds</u>.

Exercise 9

Part 1: Circle the pronouns. You may <u>circle one or more than one word in each line</u>.

1.	Tim	I	many	all	road	some
2.	we	group	this	team	mom	us
3.	walk	to	been	anyone	several	people

Part 2: Circle the words below that you are <u>allowed</u> to use in a prepositional phrase. You may <u>circle one or more than one word in each line</u>.

4.	he	whom	him	I	she
5.	you	they	her	we	it
6.	me	us	who	them	him

Part 3: In the line below each sentence, write out one part of the sentence as directed.

7. The military men met with the president to plan a strategy for the war.

   What's the <u>infinitive</u> in the above sentence? _____

8. At the end of the game the star player should have made that layup.

   What's the <u>verb</u> in the above sentence? _____

9. Thomas has never sat between Jennifer and me before.

   What's the <u>prepositional phrase</u> in the above sentence? _____

10. That missed field goal would have given my team the lead.

    Write the <u>helping verb(s)</u> from the above sentence: _____

11. I pointed to the chili powder and told my sister never to cook with that.

    What's the <u>demonstrative pronoun</u> in the above sentence? _____

12. John was being very rude during David's presentation yesterday.

    Write the <u>main verb</u> from the above sentence: _____

   If you finish early, check out the word search on the next page...

Incredible Verb Search

Verbs to find:

was walking
did run
slammed
am seeing
should leave
will be
could have been
ate
jog
must go
throw
have read
become
had
scrape
might push
would be driving

```
N U Z W H D O D L D L Z H H G
L Q E O N A N T I J J C S E N
L Q M U A X V D H V P U S M I
E B L L I W R E Z R P J L O K
D A H D E U R L R T O P A C L
L V E B N V O C H E E W M E A
J Q V E W S A G M O A Y M B W
X Y N D G S I E T N A D E L S
O C D R Q M G H L S Y N D F A
A L K I T H J S U D U I U U W
U Z F V S C R A P E L M R U C
U M W I M X T U Z C U W J T
T A I N A M S E E I N G O A Z
H T N G J L Q M R W N G P H J
N E E B E V A H D L U O C C S
```

Are you paying attention to the fact that some verbs are made up of one word and some are made up of more than one word?

3.5 – How to Find the Verb in a Sentence

A. Verbs are fairly easy to find in a sentence, but with verb phrases, it can be difficult to properly identify the <u>complete</u> verb phrase.

Here's an example:

Teacher: "Tammy, what's the verb in the following sentence?"

The boy has been fishing from the dock for three hours.

Tammy: "That's easy! The verb is *fishing*!"

Teacher: "Wrong! Looks like you're going to need to come to that three-hour extra help session this weekend."

Tammy: (weeping) "Really?"

Teacher: "Yes, really. The verb is 'has been fishing.'"

B. In order to avoid the fate awaiting Tammy, you need to be very careful when looking for the verb in a sentence.

THE VERB IS FISHING.

C. Here's a little trick you can use to narrow your search for a sentence's verb: _Make the sentence say the opposite of what's being said._

Example sentence:

In the morning Michael brushed his teeth.

D. <u>Step 1</u>: Insert a word or words that make the sentence say "the opposite":

did not brush
In the morning Michael ~~brushed~~ his teeth.

E. <u>Step 2</u>: Now go back to the original example sentence and scour <u>the general vicinity</u> where you had to make the change. This is where the verb and all of its parts (if it's a verb phrase) will be found.

F. In our example the word _brushed_ is the verb, a single-word verb.

G. Other examples:

do not love
I ~~love~~ my new pet snake.

has not been sleeping
The boy in the back row ~~has been sleeping~~ during class.

did not leave
Our delayed chartered flight finally ~~left~~ for Atlanta after three hours.

In the original sentences above, _love_ (a single-word verb), "has been sleeping" (a verb phrase), and _left_ (a single-word verb) are the verbs.

NOTE: _Please do not mistake infinitives (to + verb) for verb phrases! (See page 53 if you forget what an infinitive is.) Even though infinitives are technically verbs and are made up of more than one word, they are NOT verb phrases! For example, there is <u>no</u> verb phrase in the following sentence:_

The boy wanted to eat in the restaurant at the top of the mountain.

Exercise 10

In this exercise helping verbs play an important role.

Helping Verb Refresher Box

The following words are always helping verbs:

would	will	may
could	can	might
should		must

This next set of words are also <u>often</u> helping verbs. However, they're *not* helping verbs *all* the time. Sometimes they are main verbs in a verb phrase or even verbs all by themselves (single-word verbs).

be	are	is	have	do
been	am	was	had	does
		were	has	did

Part 1: Mark the verbs. Consider marking prepositional phrases first to make your search easier.

1. The children did sit at their desks.

2. Around the edge of the lake the geese searched for a snack.

3. The cookies inside the box have melted in the summer heat.

Part 2: In the sentences below, surround the prepositional phrases with parentheses. Verbs can never be inside a prepositional phrase, so be careful.

4. My grandfather lives with mom and me in our log cabin.

5. The grass next to the fence was growing very tall.

6. Those jets may fly in the air show on Saturday.

Part 3: Go back to sentences 4, 5, & 6 above and underline the verbs.

Part 4: *Sentence Puzzles* ✚✚✚ Compose your own sentences with different kinds of verbs. Limit your sentences to 12 words or less.

7. Use a <u>single-word verb</u> and a prepositional phrase that includes <u>two personal pronoun o.p.'s</u>. If you don't remember what a personal pronoun is, flip back to p. 27 to refresh your memory!

_____

_____

8. Use a <u>verb phrase</u> and <u>a prepositional phrase with a demonstrative pronoun as the o.p.</u> If you don't remember what a demonstrative pronoun is, flip back to p. 33 to refresh your memory!

_____

_____

9. Begin with <u>a prepositional phrase that has an indefinite pronoun for its o.p.</u>, then use a <u>single-word verb</u>. If you don't remember what an indefinite pronoun is, flip back to p. 32 to refresh your memory!

_____

_____

10. Use a <u>verb phrase</u> and <u>a prepositional phrase that includes two reflexive pronouns for o.p.'s</u>. If you don't remember what a reflexive pronoun is, flip back to p. 33 to refresh your memory!

_____

_____

11. Use a <u>single-word verb</u> and <u>a verb in the infinitive form</u>. If you don't remember what an infinitive is, flip back to p. 53 to refresh your memory!

_____

_____

12. Begin this sentence with <u>a prepositional phrase that has two personal pronoun o.p.'s</u> and then use a <u>verb phrase</u>. If you don't remember what a personal pronoun is, flip back to p. 27 to refresh your memory!

_____

_____

Humor Break!

Substitute teacher: Are you chewing gum?
Billy: No, I'm Billy Anderson.

3.6 – "Polluted" Verb Phrases

A. In many verb phrases, there is a word hidden among the helping and main verbs that is not actually part of the verb phrase. When this occurs, you might say that the verb phrase is "polluted."

   Example 1: Mark <u>may</u> **not** <u>meet</u> us at the movie tonight.

B. In "pure" verb phrases, each word is a helping verb or a form of some verb.

   Example 2: In the attic six boxes <u>will be stacked</u> near the chimney.

C. When identifying verbs in sentences, never include "polluting" words. For instance, in "Example 1" above, the verb is "may meet." The word *not* is a polluting word, and is <u>not</u> really part of the verb.

D. Here's a list of non-verbs which are often found between helping and main verbs:

     (Do **not** include these in your verb phrases!)

not	almost
never	also
still	
already	<u>most</u> words ending in –ly, like *continually* and *quietly*

   Note: These words are adverbs. We'll discuss adverbs later.

E. <u>Each word in a verb phrase must itself be a verb,</u> so don't include other types of parts of speech in a verb phrase.

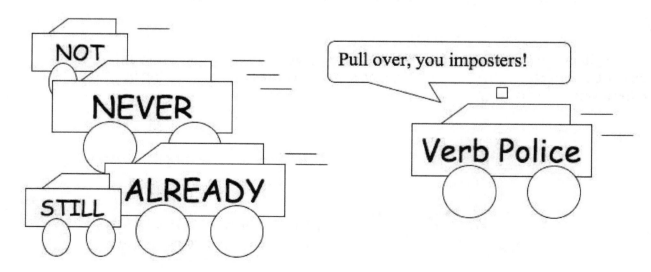

F. Look closely at the following sentence:

Bill <u>would not give</u> me a bite of his candy bar.

G. Above, look at the underlined words. Only *would* and *give* are actually verbs. You can tell because *would* is on our helping verb list, and *give* is obviously a verb because it's something you can do and it can be changed into different forms, like a past-tense form (*gave*) and an –ing form (*giving*). It also has an infinitive form, "*to give.*"

ALERT! ALERT! ALERT! ALERT!

Here is some RIIYWDN *(Really Important Information You Will Definitely Need)*:

If you are wondering if a word is a verb or even a helping verb, a good and easy test is to <u>see if it has the kinds of different forms that verbs have</u>.

For instance, all verbs have an *–ing* form: *running, thinking, tasting*, etc. They all have past tense forms, too: *cooked, built, swung, ate, danced, lived*, etc.

Even helping verbs have various forms: *can/could, will/would, may/might/must, should/shall*, etc. (Ok, fine, so *shall* isn't used much anymore, but you get the point, right?)

WATCH OUT: The word *during* is <u>not</u> a verb. *During* is a **preposition** and is an exception.

Words that are verbs or that should be included in a verb phrase have various forms, especially *–ing* and past tense forms. If a word doesn't have any other verb-like forms, do <u>not</u> include it when marking a sentence's verb.

H. In the sentence at the top of this page, *not* is <u>not</u> a verb. You can tell because there is no such word as *notting* or *notted*. Therefore, *not* cannot be part of the verb phrase. (*Not* is an adverb.)

I. The verb in the sentence at the top of this page is **"would give"** with *would* functioning as a helping verb and *give* functioning as the main verb. *Not* is a "polluting" word.

Mike <u>will slide</u> over next to Robin.

J. In the sentence above, <u>both</u> of the underlined words are forms of verbs; *will* is in our "Helping Verb Refresher Box" plus it has another form (*would*), and *slide* also has other forms as verbs do (*sliding, slid*).

K. The verb, then, is ***will slide***, with *will* functioning as a helping verb and *slide* functioning as the main verb.

L. Here are some more examples:

1. **Waiters must always treat their customers with the utmost courtesy.**

   the verb = "must treat"

   (*Always* is not a verb, so it's not included in the verb phrase. *Always* does not have various forms like verbs do, such as an *–ing* form.)

   <u>helping verb</u>: *must* (it has various forms; it behaves like a verb)

   <u>main verb</u>: *treat* (it has various forms; it behaves like a verb)

2. **On the crowded commuter train my father would never talk to anyone.**

   the verb = "would talk"

   (*never* is not a verb, so it's not included in the verb phrase. It does not have various forms like verbs do, such as an *–ing* form.)

   <u>helping verb</u>: *would* (it has various forms; it behaves like a verb)

   <u>main verb</u>: *talk* (it has various forms; it behaves like a verb)

3. **The rain should still be falling after our nap.**

   the verb = "should be falling"

   (*still* is not a verb, so it's not included in the verb phrase. It does not have various forms like verbs do, such as an *–ing* form.)

   <u>helping verbs</u>: *should, be* (both of these words have various forms; they behave like verbs)

   <u>main verb</u>: *falling* (it has various forms; it behaves like a verb)

Exercise 11

Part 1: In the blank after each sentence, write out the verb. If you find a verb phrase, <u>don't include non-verbs when you write out the verb</u>!

1. I may not be going to college soon. _____

2. In front of the house a tall tree created a huge patch of shade. _____

3. The boy between Mary and me might be sleeping. _____

4. The bus did arrive at the bus stop. _____

5. Mr. Riches is still teaching at Wonderwood Middle School. _____

Part 2: Surround prepositional phrases with parentheses. Verbs can never be inside prepositional phrases, so be careful. (Ignore the blank line after each sentence for now.)

6. Behind Thomas and her I could see three more people. _____

7. My mom went for a jog along the river walk. _____

8. I would never tell my parents a lie. _____

9. Next to my neighbor's house three purple flowers bloomed yesterday.

_____

Part 3: Go back to sentences 6, 7, 8, & 9 above and, <u>in the blank after each sentence</u>, write out the verb. If you find a verb phrase, don't include non-verbs in it!

Part 4: Compose your own sentences with different kinds of verbs. Limit your sentences to 12 words or less.

Helping Verb Refresher Box

The following words are always helping verbs:

would	will	may
could	can	might
should		must

This next set of words are also often helping verbs. However, they're not helping verbs *all* the time. Sometimes they are main verbs in a verb phrase or even verbs all by themselves (single-word verbs).

be	are	is	have	do
been	am	was	had	does
		were	has	did

10. Use a single-word verb:

_____

11. Use a verb phrase that's <u>not</u> "polluted" with a non-verb:

_____

_____

12. Use a verb phrase that <u>**is**</u> "polluted" by a non-verb:

_____

_____

Extra Practice for Evaluation 7

Part 1: Surround prepositional phrases with parentheses, AND underline verbs. Watch out for verb phrases and polluting words, and remember that verbs can never be inside prepositional phrases.

1. Under the bridge I am feeding the lonely ducks.

2. The recycling bin in the garage has already been emptied by Tim.

3. During math class I dropped my pencil on the floor.

4. On the deck in my backyard two frogs were croaking in the night.

5. My sister might never be a professional surfing champion.

Part 2: *Sentence Puzzles* ✥✚✥ Compose your own sentences using different kinds of verbs. Limit your sentences to 12 words or less.

6. Begin with a prepositional phrase and use a single-word verb. Don't forget what we talked about with intro prepositional phrases and commas!

_____

_____

7. Use a "polluted" verb phrase and three prepositional phrases:

_____

_____

8. Use a verb phrase and include a prepositional phrase that has two objects where <u>both objects are personal pronouns</u>:

_____

_____

9. Use one introductory prepositional phrase (don't forget what we talked about with intro prep. phrases and commas!) **and** a verb phrase:

_____

_____

 Evaluation 7: Finding Verbs + Single-word Verbs vs. Verb Phrases – Are you ready now?

BTW: There <u>will</u> be Personal Pronoun and Helping Verb Refresher Boxes on the test.

3.7 – Action Verbs vs. Linking Verbs

We've already mentioned how action verbs are different from linking verbs. Now here's a recap:

A. Action Verbs

Sometimes the verb tells what the subject of a sentence does, did or will be doing. This is when the verb is showing <u>action</u>. Verbs showing action are called Action Verbs.

> **Joe and Jake were playing checkers in the tent.** (The subjects, *Joe* and *Jake*, were doing something—they <u>were playing</u> checkers. So "were playing" is the verb.)

B. Linking Verbs

Other times, a subject of a sentence isn't really doing anything; instead, it is just *being* something. In this case, the verb is called a Linking Verb because it <u>links</u> the subject to something it is being.

> **The waves near the reef were incredible.** (*Waves* is the subject and *incredible* is what the subject was being—these words are linked by the verb, *were*, an action verb.)

> **The coach has been unhappy with the team's performance.** (*Coach* is the subject and *unhappy* is what the subject was being—these words are linked by this sentence's verb, "has been," a linking verb.)

C.
As stated earlier, one of the most important things someone can learn regarding grammar is recognizing the difference between action verbs and linking verbs. Understanding many other grammar concepts will rely on your ability to tell the difference between action and linking verbs.

D.
Most importantly, however, is that <u>action verbs make for better writing</u>, so if you can find linking verbs in your own writing, you can get rid of them!

How to Tell the Difference Between Linking Verbs & Action Verbs

A. Once you find a sentence's verb, there are four strategies you can use to tell if the verb is action or linking:

Strategy 1 **Use your common sense**: Is something happening in the sentence? Is the verb you've found something you could <u>do</u>? Is the verb you've found an "action-ee" kind of word? Remember, action verbs involve mental, emotional, and physical actions.

If the answer to any of the above questions is "yes," then you probably have an action verb. If not, the verb is most likely linking.

☼ *ALWAYS* apply your **common sense** *first*!

(Your common sense is a terrible thing to waste!)

Strategy 2 **The classics**: Know the "classic" linking verbs, verbs that are *always* linking. If the verb (or <u>main</u> verb of a verb phrase) is one of these, then you obviously have a linking verb.

The "classic" linking verbs are:

a. Any form of the verb "to be": *am, are, is, was, were, be, been, being*

b. Any form of the verb "to seem": *seem, seems, seemed*

c. Any form of the verb "to become": *become, becomes, became, becoming* *

<u>NOTE</u>: When applying this strategy to verb phrases, look at the <u>main</u> verb—the <u>last</u> word in the verb phrase.

* **See appendix regarding an exception—it's possible, but rare, for "to become" to be an action verb.**

Exercise 12: Mark the verbs in the following sentences.

Mark action verbs with a box:

At home I ⌐colored¬ on the wall.

Mark linking verbs with an "L" shape:

The boys ⌞have been⌟ there.

Reminder: If you find a verb phrase, be careful—do <u>not</u> include non-verbs in it!

Example:

After an hour the alarm ⌐was s̶t̶i̶l̶l̶ ringing.¬

1. The team on the bus is leaving for a tournament in California.

2. The puzzles in that book seem easy to me.

3. On Tuesday you should try the spaghetti for lunch.

4. The horse leaped over the fence near the grandstand.

5. The weather may not become nicer over the weekend.

6. The apple pie was on the kitchen counter this morning.

7. I have been to Spain to see a bullfight.

8. In the wind the trees were bending wildly.

A closer look:

A. How many sentences above have "classic" linking verbs? _____

B. How many sentences above have verb phrases? _____

C. Which sentence above has a "polluting" word in it? _____

Some more strategies—ones you may need if you get into a pinch!

Strategy 3 **Replace the verb**: Replace the verb or verb phrase with a "classic" linking verb. This is a very good and popular strategy.

Examples:

> **This soup tastes delicious.**

Replace the verb *tastes* with a form of the verb "to be," like *is/was*, *are/were*—whichever form of the verb best fits, such as

> **is**
> **This soup ~~tastes~~ delicious.**

If the meaning of the sentence does <u>not change</u>, as in the sentence above, then the original verb (*tastes*) is a <u>linking</u> verb.

Here's another example:

> **are**
> **The children ~~were having~~ a great time at the party.**

In this example, the meaning of the sentence <u>changes</u> when we replace the original verb, "were having," with the classic linking verb *are*, so "were having" is an <u>action</u> verb.

Strategy 4 **Sentence structure**: You can also look at the structure of the sentence. Draw a vertical line right after the verb and look at the words to the right of your line.

In linking verb sentences, after the verb you will often find a word that describes the subject of the sentence. *In action verb sentences there will <u>not</u> be anything after the verb that describes the subject.*

Examples:

> **In the afternoon the weather was becoming | really nasty.**

After the verb "was becoming," you can see the word *nasty* which describes the subject *weather*. Therefore, "was becoming" is a <u>linking</u> verb.

> **Johnny ran | three miles on the track yesterday.**

After the verb *ran* there is no word that describes the subject *Johnny*. Therefore, *ran* is an <u>action</u> verb.

 **Exercise 13**

Part 1: Surround prepositional phrases with parentheses. Verbs can never be inside prepositional phrases, so be careful.

1. I will probably buy three pieces of pizza at lunch.

2. She may come to your house after school next week.

3. Our new puppy snuggled between me and my dad on the couch.

4. He seemed very tall for a sixth grader.

5. In front of my house my sister parked the car.

6. Most of the guests should be on time for the ceremony tonight.

7. The celebrity chef expertly spread the icing on the vanilla cake.

8. During the speech many audience members appeared sleepy.

9. He paused for a moment at the stop sign.

10. I am not happy about this grade!

Part 2: Go back to sentences 1 - 10 above and mark action verbs with a box and linking verbs with an "L" shape. **Reminder:** If you find a verb phrase, be careful—do <u>not</u> include non-verbs in it!

SCHOLAR ZONE

The earliest speakers of what would become the English language were northern Europeans who invaded England in the 5th and 6th centuries AD (CE), after the Roman Empire collapsed. They were from various tribes, including the Angles, Saxons, Jutes, Franks, and Frisians, but we have come to refer to them generally as the "Anglo-Saxons."

English, or "Anglish," was a combination of the assorted Germanic languages these invaders spoke. English also gradually adopted the Latin alphabet the Romans had earlier brought to Britain. A new language had been born, a language with a Latin alphabet and heavy with Germanic words, but not nearly finished!

Over the next several hundred years, many new words would enter the language, and spellings and pronunciations would be adjusted. Old English would be very tough for a modern-day English speaker to read. Then came Middle English, and finally Modern English in the 16th century. Modern English has continued to evolve, but 16th century English, which is the English William Shakespeare used, can be read fairly easily by today's English speakers.

Warning... Super Scholar Zone! Any idea how *England* got its name?

Tricky Verbs

A. Two more things worth noting here concerning action and linking verbs:

B. The verb "to have," for some reason, appears to a lot of people to be a linking verb. But as main verbs or single-word verbs <u>all forms of the verb "to have" are ACTION verbs</u>.

> **He has a huge headache.** (*Has* is the verb, and it's an ACTION verb.)

> **We will be having turkey for dinner tonight.** ("Will be having" is the verb, and since the main verb is a form of the verb "to have," "will be having" is an ACTION verb.)

C. The "sense" words—*look, feel, sound, taste,* and *smell*—can be linking **or** action verbs depending on how they are used. Of course they look like sure action verbs, but <u>many times they are not action verbs</u>.

> **The chef tasted the soup.** (*Tasted* is an <u>action</u> verb here because the subject, *chef*, is actually doing something.)

> **The soup tasted delicious.** (In this sentence, *tasted* is a <u>linking</u> verb because the subject, *soup*, isn't doing anything—it's just <u>being</u> delicious.)

D. Below, check the box next to the sentence where *looks* is an <u>Action</u> Verb:

☐ **That dress looks really fancy.**

☐ **My mom always looks through the sale rack first.**

Did you check the right box?

This is a VERY IMPORTANT page—you should bookmark it and be sure to review it before the next evaluation!

⚡ **Exercise 14**

Part 1: Surround prepositional phrases with parentheses. Verbs can never be inside prepositional phrases so be careful.

1. I did receive several awards at my graduation.

2. Until noon all of the burgers will be served by the Girl Scouts.

3. Against all odds my team won the championship of our league.

4. On the sidelines the coach looked terribly nervous.

5. At the game you might feel chilly without a coat or a hat.

6. After college Tommy would soon become a great scientist.

7. Jill can take a seat by them along the aisle.

8. Over the break I will have my twelfth birthday party at the beach.

9. To Melinda and me the test seemed really tough.

10. That goat may not eat the food from your hand.

Part 2: Go back to sentences 1 - 10 above and mark action verbs with a box and linking verbs with an "L" shape. **Reminder:** If you find a verb phrase, be careful—do <u>not</u> include non-verbs in it!

SCHOLAR ZONE

Many, many words from the ancient Anglo-Saxon language, or Old English, actually remain in Modern English. Several days of the week, for instance, were named after the gods of these ancient people, including Tuesday (Tiw's Day; Tiw was their god of battle), Wednesday (Woden's Day for Woden, the god of war), Thursday (Thor's Day for Thor, the god of thunder), and Friday (Frigg's Day for Frigg, the goddess of love).

Cool, huh? You can read about these gods and goddesses if you check out a book about Norse mythology.

(Do you know where the terms Saturday, Sunday, and Monday come from? Hint: The men from Latium.)

Extra Practice for Evaluation 8

Part 1: Surround prepositional phrases with parentheses in sentences 1 - 5. Verbs can never be inside prepositional phrases so be careful.

1. The snake slid through the grass near the porch.

2. Everyone on my bus laughed loudly at my hilarious joke.

3. The pencils under the desk were spilled by Melissa.

4. Your sandwich from the deli is next to that soda can.

5. The weeds along the fence have grown to my knees.

Part 2: In the sentences above <u>as well as</u> the sentences below…

mark action verbs with a box: At home I colored on the wall.

mark linking verbs with an "L" shape: The boys had never been there.

6. In front of the room Jimmy did find three large tables.

7. I had never run a race against you.

8. The napkins do not have pretty flower designs on them.

9. Ten jellybeans might be rolling around under the table.

10. During the movie children had quietly sipped their sodas.

11. To Maude and me everyone at the school seemed very polite.

12. Must you bother us during this TV show?

13. This award can be presented to Julia and him on Sunday.

Part 3: Compose your own sentences with different kinds of verbs. Limit your sentences to 12 words or less.

14. Use a verb phrase that is a linking verb:

_____

_____

15. *Sentence Puzzle* ✢✛✢ Use a single-word verb that is an action verb, and <u>include a prepositional phrase that has two personal pronoun o.p.'s</u>:

_____

_____

16. Use a single-word verb that is a linking verb:

_____

_____

17. Use a verb phrase that is an action verb:

_____

_____

Part 4: List the four strategies you can use to determine if a verb is action or linking:

18. _____

19. _____

20. _____

21. _____

➤ **Evaluation 8: Action Verb vs. Linking Verb + Single-word Verbs vs. Verb Phrases** – Are you ready now?

BTW: There <u>will</u> be a Helping Verb Refresher Box <u>and</u> a Personal Pronoun Refresher Box on the test.

Chapter 4

Thinking Carefully About the Verbs in Your Writing

4.1 – Introduction to Verbs & Writing

Now that you've had some experience with verbs in a grammatical way, it's time to use that experience to improve your writing! Good writers are very good with their verbs. They know how powerful good verb usage is. So, what are the most-important things to learn about verb usage?

There are three main ways a person can improve his or her writing through attention to verbs:

1. **Limit the use of helping verbs.**

2. **Use action verbs rather than linking verbs** whenever possible.

3. **Use the "active voice" in your writing.** In other words, when using action verbs, make sure that the main person or thing your sentence is about is doing the action.

Humor Break!

The teacher asked the little girl if she was going to the dance. "No, I ain't going" was the reply.

The teacher corrected the child: "You must not say, 'I ain't going,' you must say, 'I am not going.' " She continued in order to impress the point: "I am not going. He is not going. We are not going. You are not going. They are not going. Now, dear, can you say all that?"

The little girl nodded and smiled brightly. "Sure!" she replied. "There ain't nobody going!"

4.2 – Limiting the Use of Helping Verbs

A. Helping verbs are often unnecessary. Consider the underlined verbs in the following sentences:

>   1. **As Tom slept, the cat <u>was napping</u> on the window sill.**

>   2. **As Tom slept, the cat <u>napped</u> on the window sill.**

Is there any difference in meaning between sentences 1 and 2?

Good writers know that using extra, unnecessary words is a no-no! Therefore, sentence #2 above is <u>better writing</u> than sentence #1.

B. Helping verbs are necessary sometimes. They can help put verbs into just the right tense. In one of the sentences below, the helping verb *has* plays an important role.

>   1. **Sheila <u>has run</u> in many marathons.**

>   2. **Sheila <u>runs</u> in many marathons.**

<u>Sentence 1</u> states that Sheila has, in the past, run marathons. It also implies that she may or may not run marathons anymore.

<u>Sentence 2</u> states that Sheila has run and still runs marathons.

C. The point is to recognize helping verbs in your writing and eliminate them whenever it's possible to do so.

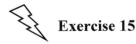 **Exercise 15**

<u>Directions</u>: Read the following passage. If you notice any unnecessary helping verbs (or other unnecessary words), cross them out. You may need to adjust the endings of verbs, too.

Yesterday, Hugh was running in the park when he noticed something shiny that was sitting on one of the park benches along his route. He didn't think much of it, but when he had returned to his apartment, his curiosity about the object he had seen glimmering on that park bench was beginning to really bother him. He decided to go back and check it out.

As he was approaching the bench, he noticed that an old woman was now sitting on the bench near where he had seen the shiny object. He was wondering if the object had belonged to her. Suddenly, she stood up, turned, and, with a huge smile on her face, walked off. Her clothes were tattered and filthy, but a giant diamond ring was sparkling on her left hand!

©Richbaub's
Ink Works

4.3 – Using Action Verbs Rather Than Linking Verbs

A. Beginning writers often over-use linking verbs like *was*, *is*, *were*, *are*, etc. Avoiding the over-use of such words should be a goal for all writers.

B. Linking verbs relate information in the least visual way. Writing comes alive when authors use words that plant images in readers' minds.

For example:

> **1. Joe <u>was</u> at the bus stop for twenty minutes.**

> **2. Joe <u>stood</u> at the bus stop for twenty minutes.**

Above, the verb *stood* relays an image to the reader. It's not an incredibly descriptive word, but the word *was* relates <u>nothing</u>, and the reader is left to wonder if Joe is standing, sitting, pacing, laughing, jumping, or whatever… Don't force your readers to do all of this wondering!

C. Some verbs are better than others. Even some action verbs are over-used. Your challenge as a writer is to pick the verb that most-accurately describes to your reader what you see in your mind when you're composing your sentences.

For example:

> **1. Jaclyn took a book from her locker and ran to class.**

> **2. Jaclyn grabbed a book from her locker and ran to class.**

Above, both sentences have action verbs. Which sentence is better? Why?

D. In summary, limiting linking verbs and choosing interesting action verbs WILL improve your writing!

Exercise 16

Part 1: In the following sentences <u>cross out the linking verbs and replace them with action verbs</u>. You may need to cross out more than just the linking verb in some sentences, and in some cases you may even have to add a few words.

1. This morning Tara was in the backyard.

2. The guests were upset at their waiter.

3. The summer sun is high in the sky at noon.

4. Under the waves near the beach were schools of silver fish.

5. During the lecture several students became very sleepy.

Part 2: In the following sentences put a box around each verb (they're all action verbs). In the spaces under each sentence, suggest **better action verbs** that could replace the original verbs. **If you can also eliminate helping verbs, then do so.**

6. Behind the security guard the thief was walking toward the vault.

_____ , _____ , _____

7. Manny looked through his notebook for his missing assignment.

_____ , _____ , _____

8. On Fridays we usually have pizza for dinner.

_____ , _____ , _____

9. Will you please get that hat for me?

_____ , _____ , _____

10. In the wild, wolves will follow their prey sometimes for days.

_____ , _____ , _____

SCHOLAR ZONE

As the new English language worked out its kinks during its early years, one thing to think about was if there were enough letters to represent all of the sounds people were using. After all, the Runic alphabet had quite a few more letters and sounds than the Roman Latin alphabet.

Some sounds unique to the old Runic alphabet faded out of English, but some remained and so more letters were added to the Roman alphabet that English speakers had adopted. A couple of additional letters were added over time to clarify similar or confusing spellings and pronunciations.

Runic	ᚠ ᛒ ᛣ ᚼ ᛉ ᛗ ᚹ ᚷ ᚻ ᛁ ᛚ ᛁ ᛗ ᚾ ᚠ ᛈ ᚱ ᚢ ᛏ ᛖ ᚹ ᛦ ᛚ ᛋ ᚠ ᛏ ᛏ ᚩ ᛁ ᚦ ᛪ
Early Latin	A B C D E F B I K L M N O P Q R S T V X Æ Œ
Roman Latin	A B C D E F G H I L M N O P Q R S T V X Y Z
Modern English	A B C D E F G H I J K L M N O P Q R S T U V W X Y Z

Write your name out in...

     Runic:

     Early Latin:

     Modern English:

Which version of your name do you like best??

4.4 – Using the Active Voice in Your Writing

A. When using action verbs, **make sure that the main person or thing your sentence is about (the subject) is doing the action**.

For example:

    1. The <u>ball was kicked</u> through the goalposts by Junior.

The focus (subject) of sentence 1 is the ball, but the ball didn't do anything—something was done <u>to</u> it. It was Junior who actually did something. Therefore, Junior and what he did should be the focus of this sentence, as they are in sentence 2:

    2. <u>Junior kicked</u> the ball through the goalposts.

B. Above, sentence 1 is an example of "passive voice" writing. Sentence 2 is written in the preferable "active voice." Active voice means that the subject of the sentence is actually doing something.

C. You may notice that when you pay attention to eliminating helping verbs, you sometimes end up changing a sentence around from passive to active voice.

Examples:

Passive Voice:

Dinner <u>was served</u> to us by a bearded man in a velvet jacket.

Active Voice:

A bearded man in a velvet jacket <u>served</u> us dinner.

D. So think "active voice" when writing. Create sentences where the subjects actually <u>do</u> something!

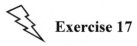 **Exercise 17**

Part 1: Write "A" or "P" in the blank before each sentence depending on whether the sentence is written in the active (A) or passive (P) voice.

_____ 1. The baby frog was handed to Mike by the science teacher.

_____ 2. During the thunderstorm the child cried for his mommy.

_____ 3. The surfer was easily flipped over by the massive wave.

_____ 4. Mary planted a giant sunflower outside her bedroom window.

Part 2: Using the given verbs and prepositional phrases, construct sentences written in the <u>active voice</u>. Try to limit your sentences to 12 words or less, and don't forget to try to avoid using any helping verbs.

5. chased   up the tree

_____

_____

6. hit   over the fence

_____

_____

7. protected   in the cedar chest

_____

_____

8. planned   by my parents

_____

_____

Incredible Crossword Puzzle

Complete the puzzle to review some of the terms we've studied so far...

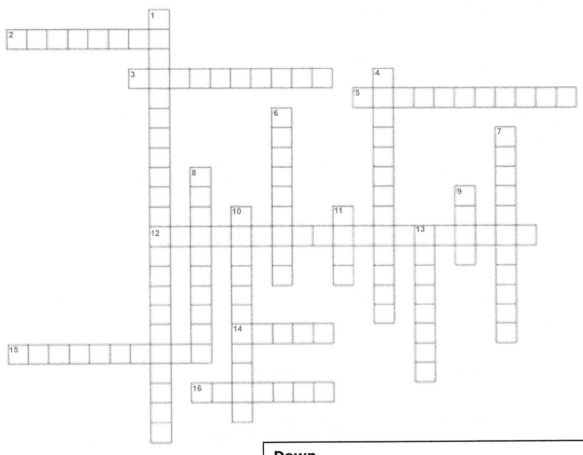

Down

1. the last word in a prepositional phrase
4. imagine pointing when trying to remember *these* (a type of pronoun!)
6. the pronouns that end with *–selves* or *–self*
7. begins a phrase that ends with an o.p.
8. this pronoun type includes words like *everyone*, *many*, *several*, and *few*
9. tells you what the subject is doing, or links subject to a word that describes what the subject is being
10. a connecting word, such as *and* or *but*
11. person, place, thing, or idea
13. these pronouns have rules—some can be used in prepositional phrases and some cannot

Across

2. in a verb phrase, the last word
3. a verb that's composed of more than one word
5. helps a main verb get into the right tense
12. a group of words beginning with a preposition and ending with a noun or pronoun
14. try not to use one after a single introductory prepositional phrase
15. *to* plus a verb
16. subs in for a noun sometimes

Chapter 5

The Key to Clarity: All About the Subjects of Sentences

5.1 – Introduction to Subjects

There are plenty of punctuation and usage rules that require an understanding of subjects. For instance, certain pronouns can never be used as subjects. Did you know that you can never use me *as a subject?*

In addition, as you become a more advanced writer, you will learn all about phrases and clauses, and the major difference between a phrase and a clause is that one has a subject and *a verb and one doesn't.*

How about this: Do you know what a compound sentence is? You should, because there is an important punctuation situation involved with compound sentences—and knowing about subjects is a key to recognizing a compound sentence.

A. As stated earlier, a subject is the main person or thing a sentence is about. Subjects are always nouns or pronouns.

B. Most sentences have one subject, but many have two subjects, and some sentences have three or more.

Examples:

1. The test in social studies is very difficult.
Subject = *test*

2. My aunt and uncle live in New Jersey.
Subjects = *aunt, uncle* (The word "and" is not part of the subject—it's one of those connecting words called <u>conjunctions</u>.)

3. Around the corner two thieves are robbing a bank!
Subject = *thieves*

4. My ankles, feet, and toes were sore after the marathon.
Subjects = *ankles, feet, toes*

Can you pick out the <u>verbs</u> in the sentences above?	Can you tell if they are action or linking verbs? (Circle one.)
1. _____	AV LV
2. _____	AV LV
3. _____	AV LV
4. _____	AV LV

5.2 – The Relationship Between Subjects & Verbs

A. Subjects "belong" to verbs. The subject is the person or thing that is doing or being what the verb says.

B. Do you remember how to find the <u>verb</u>? Make the sentence say the opposite... (See p. 56.)

C. To find a verb's <u>subject</u>, first locate the verb, then ask, "Who or what _____?"

(insert verb)

Examples:

    1. At the picnic on Saturday everyone loved **the fried chicken.**

        "Who or what <u>loved</u>?" Answer = *everyone*, so *everyone* is the subject

    2. My grandmother sat **near the window in her room.**

        "Who or what <u>sat</u>?" Answer = *grandmother*, so *grandmother* is the subject

    3. The brother and sister had **similar smiles.**

        "Who or what <u>had</u>?" Answer = *brother*, *sister*

    4. The construction workers are **at the corner of my block.**

        "Who or what <u>are</u>?" Answer = *workers*

D. Notice that the subject in #4 above is NOT "construction workers." How come?

    Subjects are nouns and pronouns <u>only</u>—they do NOT include things that <u>describe</u> the subject... *Construction* describes the noun *workers*, so *construction* is **not** part of the subject.

E. Also, subjects are NEVER inside prepositional phrases. What's the subject in the following sentence?

At the restaurant all of the boys ordered fried chicken.

Write your answer here: _____   (Were you correct?)

Part 1: Surround prepositional phrases with parentheses.

1. Beneath a layer of snow three little eggs were found by Michael.

2. The woman near my dad and me did carry three large bundles.

3. At night she and I would never watch movies about scary things.

4. A snake might slowly slither between the rocks at my feet.

5. The sky should become dark before the rainfall.

Part 2: In the sentences above, mark action verbs with boxes and linking verbs with "L" shapes. Be careful of "polluted" verb phrases, and do you remember that verbs are <u>never</u> found inside prepositional phrases?

Part 3: Now circle the subjects in the sentences—but be careful because, like verbs, subjects are NEVER found inside prepositional phrases.

Part 4: Circle the subjects in the sentences below. Remember, subjects are NEVER found inside prepositional phrases.

6. On the mountain top a coyote will often howl at the moon.

7. I am going to the beach with Michael.

8. None of the boys in the back row are very tall kids.

9. For example, the girls are standing in the front of the line.

10. Does our p.e. coach require us to run three laps on Mondays?

Humor Break!

"I don't need none," shouted the lady of the house even before the young man at the door had a chance to say anything.

"How do you know, lady?" he said. "I just might be selling grammar books."

5.3 – Locating Subjects in Sentences

A. It's important to begin to pay attention to sentence patterns!

B. For example, verbs are usually in the middle of a sentence, so when you're looking for verbs, look there.

C. As far as subjects are concerned, most come <u>before</u> the verb. Understanding basic sentence patterns will save you time when analyzing the parts of a sentence.

D. Also, subjects and prepositional phrases don't mix! Subjects are NEVER inside prepositional phrases.

E. Therefore, before you set out to locate a sentence's subject, surround each prepositional phrase so that you know not to look there. Many times, if you mark the prepositional phrases, there aren't too many words left that could be the subject which makes your search for the subject easier.

Some common sentence "formulas":

$$(\quad) + S + V + (\quad)$$

$$S + (\quad) + V + (\quad)$$

$$S + V + (\quad) + (\quad)$$

Exercise 19

Part 1: Surround prepositional phrases with parentheses.

1. Everyone in my class is doing well on the math tests.

2. For many people thunder can sound scary.

3. Mary and James would never have their homework on time.

4. Most of the questions on the test were really easy.

5. The present from her and him must have been wrapped by their mom.

Part 2: In the sentences above, mark action verbs with boxes and linking verbs with "L" shapes. Be careful of "polluted" verb phrases, and do you remember that verbs are never found inside prepositional phrases?

Part 3: Now circle the subjects in the sentences—but be careful because, like verbs, subjects are NEVER found inside prepositional phrases.

Part 4: Circle the subjects in the sentences below. Remember, subjects are NEVER found inside prepositional phrases.

6. Several of my friends may come over to my house over the weekend.

7. Sarah and I haven't met the new family across the street.

8. The gas station does glow on the deserted midnight highway.

9. Between my dad and me crept a greasy little rat.

10. Do you or your brother ever read in your beds at night?

Extra Practice for Evaluation 9

Part 1: Surround prepositional phrases with parentheses, then mark action verbs with boxes and linking verbs with "L" shapes. Verbs can never be inside prepositional phrases so be careful.

1. At nap time she sat on the bed and comforted the tiny baby.

2. For a long time the line did not move at all.

3. My aunt and uncle gave giant beach towels to my brother and me.

4. The sound seemed to fade in the distance.

5. You or I have never had a turtle in a box for a pet.

6. The greyhounds should be chasing the bunny around the track.

Part 2: In sentences 1-6, circle the subjects. Remember: Subjects are never found inside prepositional phrases.

Part 3: *Sentence Puzzles* ✚✚✚ Write sentences as directed. Limit your sentences to 15 words or less.

7. Begin with a prepositional phrase, and use a <u>verb phrase that is a linking verb</u>:

_____

_____

8. Use a <u>single-word verb that is a linking verb</u> and two prepositional phrases:

_____

_____

9. Use a "<u>polluted</u>" <u>verb phrase that is an action verb</u>, and include three prepositional phrases:

_____

_____

 Evaluation 9: Subjects + Action Verbs vs. Linking Verbs – Are you ready now?

BTW: There will be a "Classic" Linking Verbs Refresher Box on the Test

5.4 – Personal Pronouns & Subjects

A. As you know, a subject is either a noun or a pronoun. But what you might not know is that there are rules for using certain pronouns as subjects.

B. Do you remember when we discussed Personal Pronouns and prepositional phrases? Well, it's those Personal Pronouns again. Some can <u>never</u> be used as subjects.

C. Once more, here are the Personal Pronouns:

Objective Case Personal Pronouns	Nominative Case Personal Pronouns
me	I
you	you
her	she
it	it
him	he
us	we
them	they
whom	who

> Do the phrases
> **Mr. Tummes**
> and
> **TIE EYE UO**
> ring a bell?

As you can see, *you* and *it* are all purpose personal pronouns.

D. What's most important here is that when using Personal Pronouns as subjects, you MUST choose a word from the <u>Nominative Case</u> Personal Pronouns list.

E. This is different than for prepositional phrases—in prepositional phrases you must use only <u>Objective Case</u> Personal Pronouns.

F. For subjects you may **only** use <u>Nominative Case</u> Personal Pronouns.

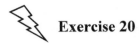 **Exercise 20**

In this exercise you will use personal pronouns.

Personal Pronoun Refresher Box

Objective Case Personal Pronouns	Nominative Case Personal Pronouns
me	I
you	you
her	she
it	it
him	he
us	we
them	they
whom	who

As you can see, *you* and *it* are all-purpose personal pronouns.

Part 1: *Sentence Puzzles* ✚╫✚ Write sentences as directed.

Write two sentences that each have a personal pronoun for a subject <u>and</u> a prepositional phrase with a personal pronoun o.p. (object of the preposition). Limit your sentences to 12 words or less.

1. _____

_____

2. **(Use a verb phrase in this sentence.)** _____

_____

Write two sentences that each have two subjects where BOTH are personal pronouns. Limit your sentences to 12 words or less.

3. _____

_____

4. **(Use a <u>polluted</u> verb phrase in this sentence.)** _____

_____

Part 2: Fill in the blanks with personal pronouns. Don't use *you* or *it*—that would be too easy!

5. _____ and my dad enjoy fishing on Saturday mornings.

6. After school _____ and _____ are going shopping at the mall.

7. _____ and _____ were excited about making the baseball team.

8. At the beach Joe and _____ were playing in a volleyball tournament.

Part 3: In the sentences below, fix any personal pronouns used incorrectly.

9. Toward the end of the day Joe and him headed for the swimming pool.

10. The spider landed in front of she and Judy.

11. Neither of the boys will have cake with Tommy and I.

12. By who will you sit during the music festival this afternoon?

5.5 – Multiple Subjects, Multiple Verbs, & Compound Sentences

A. The following sentences both have two subjects and two verbs, but they are very different kinds of sentences.

    a. Jill and her sister stopped at a restaurant and ate dinner.

    b. David needed some bread, but the grocery store had already closed.

B. The main difference between the two sentences above is that in sentence "a" the verbs <u>share</u> the <u>same</u> subjects, while in sentence "b" each verb has <u>its very own subject</u>.

C. Sentence "b" is called a **compound sentence** because it is really two <u>separate sentences that have been joined together</u>.

D. Which of the following sentences are <u>compound</u> sentences?

    1. The water rose and washed away my sand castle.

    2. My jeans got dirty, so I put them in the laundry.

    3. Meredith has excellent grades, and she is a fabulous soccer player.

    4. In front of my house a truck lost control and skidded into a ditch.

SCHOLAR ZONE

Most of the most basic words in English, such as personal pronouns and prepositions, come from German origin through the language of the Anglo-Saxons.

Examples of the thousands of other Anglo-Saxon words we still use today include words like *rain, man, fear, bed, land, drink, sun, moon, house, eat,* and *milk*.

As children, English language speakers use mostly these Anglo-Saxon, or Old English, words. But English is a language influenced and enlarged by many other languages since its birth!

As we grow older, Latin words (*project, interrupt, contain*) slip into our vocabulary, as do Greek (*atlas, biology, democracy*), French (*chef, machine, café*), and more (*taco, spaghetti, cilantro, bagel, banana*)!

Punctuating Compound Sentences

A. It's important to be able to recognize compound sentences because there's a punctuation rule for them:

> **When you join two separate sentences together to form a compound sentence, you must use either <u>a comma and a conjunction</u> OR <u>a semi-colon</u> to make the connection.**

FYI

- Sentences joined without punctuation are called **"run-on"** sentences.
- A **"comma splice"** error is where sentences are joined with *only* a comma.

B. Most often, a compound sentence is formed with a comma and one of the following conjunctions

for
and
nor
but
or
yet
so

> The word *for* is a conjunction when it's being used to connect sentences. When it begins a prepositional phrase, it's a preposition.

C. These connecting words are called **coordinating conjunctions** and are often referred to by the acronym "fanboys" as their first letters spell this out.

D. Once again, connect two sentences with <u>a comma and a conjunction</u> OR <u>a semi-colon</u>:

   a. My soup was too hot**, so** I put an ice cube in it.

   b. Basketball is a fun sport**, but** it is very tiring.

   c. My sister ordered a sandwich**, and** my dad ordered a salad.

   d. Our neighbors traveled to Disney World**;** my family stayed home.

E. When a sentence has more than one subject and/or more than one verb but is <u>not</u> compound, do NOT use a comma and a conjunction or a semi-colon:

   1. The skydiver jumped out of the plane and tumbled toward the earth.

   2. The snakes at the zoo frightened my mom and gave me nightmares!

   3. Thomas and his dog jumped out of the car and headed for the beach.

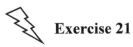 **Exercise 21**

Part 1: Write two compound sentences. Limit each sentence to 15 words or less, and <u>be sure to use the correct punctuation.</u>

1. _____

_____

2. **(Use a verb phrase in this sentence.)** _____

_____

Part 2: Insert commas or semi-colons where needed. Some sentences will not need any punctuation added. On the line after each sentence, explain why you added or did not add punctuation. (Write "it's a compound sentence" or "it's not compound.")

3. Before the game I stretched my legs and warmed up my arm.

_____

4. Tina's uncle bought two Super Bowl tickets and gave them to Tina and me.

_____

5. The bear cubs looked lost hopefully their mother will find them soon.

_____

6. We needed a time out for our defense looked confused.

_____

7. In the cabinet next to the refrigerator I may find some cereal and pour myself a bowl.

_____

8. He and I will be on the same flight so we will arrive in Orlando together.

_____

Extra Practice for Evaluation 10

Part 1: Surround prepositional phrases with parentheses, mark action verbs with boxes and linking verbs with "L" shapes, AND circle subjects.

1. For summer vacation you should always go to the beach.

2. My dad and I played soccer against the neighborhood kids.

3. Some of my teammates were wearing long blue socks.

4. I travelled down the road, and I saw three turtles in a pond.

5. Those burgers on the grill smell delicious.

6. The problems on page six seem too difficult for me and Mike.

Part 2: Fix personal pronouns used incorrectly.

7. The alligator slowly crawled toward my mom and I.

8. The Walkers and us arrived before Lisa and him.

9. From Los Angeles we drove north for a scenic journey with she and my uncle.

Part 3: Insert commas or semi-colons if needed.

10. Around eight o'clock we went to the porch and my mom made us a cup of hot chocolate.

11. Sally and Terrence joined the team and quickly became our best players.

12. For lunch we had grilled cheese sandwiches we didn't have time for dessert.

Part 4: *Sentence Puzzles* ✚✚✚ Write sentences as directed.

13. Write a compound sentence that includes three prepositional phrases (not necessarily in a row!) and two <u>different</u> verb phrases.

_____

_____

14. Write a sentence that includes one verb and two subjects where <u>BOTH subjects are personal pronouns</u>.

_____

_____

15. Write a sentence that includes two verbs and a prepositional phrase with two <u>personal pronoun</u> o.p.'s.

_____

_____

BTW: There <u>will</u> be a personal pronoun refresher box on the test.

 **Evaluation 10: Finding Subjects, Using Personal Pronouns as Subjects +
Punctuating Compound Sentences** – Are you ready now?

Chapter 6

Introduction to Participial Phrases & Appositives

If you take a look at your own writing, you will notice that your sentences all look pretty similar. You begin with a subject, follow with a verb, and throw in a prepositional phrase or two here and there.

As your writing becomes more sophisticated, however, you will include some other elements, such as subordinate clauses and new kinds of phrases. Building your sentences with things besides subjects, verbs, and prepositional phrases creates better sentence variety, and good writers definitely construct sentences in a variety of ways and with a variety of elements.

Two of the easiest new elements you can add to your sentences to create better sentence variety are "participial phrases" and "appositives," and that's what this chapter is all about! Knowing about these writing elements will also teach you a little bit more about using commas properly, so it's very practical stuff.

6.1 – What Is a Phrase?

A. You've become quite familiar with prepositional phrases by now, which is a great way to begin your study of the details of the English language. But do you know what the word *phrase* actually means?

B. A phrase is a group of words that expresses an idea but does not include a subject-verb pair.

C. Consider this prepositional <u>phrase</u>: "in the window"

This phrase definitely expresses an idea, but it definitely is NOT a sentence. You'd have to add some things to create a sentence.

D. What's a "sentence" anyway? Well, a sentence must have a subject and a verb (a subject-verb pair), AND it must express a complete thought.

The cat sat in the window.

Now <u>that</u> is a sentence!

E. Again, a <u>phrase</u> is definitely NOT a sentence. Check out the following phrases:

"wrapped up"   "over the barn"   "washing a car"

"sitting at the table"   "with my dad"   "into the wall"

"the tree in my backyard"   "a great student"

A phrase **is a group of words that expresses an idea but does <u>not</u> include a subject-verb pair.**

F. Hmm… Some of the phrases above are not prepositional phrases, are they?

Circle the phrases above that are NOT simply prepositional phrases.

G. Yes, folks, there are other kinds of phrases besides prepositional phrases!

(And, most importantly, using them <u>will</u> improve your writing!)

SCHOLAR ZONE

The way a word is pronounced can give away a word's origin. For example, compare how "ch" is pronounced in the following English language words:

chimney, chase, charm (Anglo-Saxon origin)

chef, chauffer, chivalry (French origin)

chronic, stomach, choir (Greek origin)

6.2 – Participial Phrases

A. Check out the <u>underlined phrases</u> that begin the following sentences:

1. <u>Running like mad from the defender,</u> the quarterback threw a desperate pass to his favorite receiver.

2. <u>Slowed by the heavy traffic,</u> Mark would arrive late to his grandma's house.

3. <u>Talking quickly,</u> my mom told the nurse about my accident.

 Each of the underlined groups of words above is something called a **participial** phrase.

Beginning a sentence with a participial phrase is a GREAT way to create a new kind of sentence.

B. A **participial phrase** is a phrase (a group of words without a subject-verb pair) that begins with an *–ing* or *–ed* verb. A participial phrase is a **descriptive** phrase. <u>When it comes at the beginning of the sentence,</u> a participial phrase describes the subject of the sentence.

<u>Slowed by the heavy traffic,</u> **Mark** would arrive late to his grandma's house.

C. Participial phrases can actually come anywhere in a sentence:

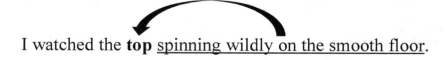

I watched the **top** <u>spinning wildly on the smooth floor.</u>

D. For now let's keep it simple and just try to add some variety to our sentence *beginnings* by <u>starting</u> some sentences with *–ing* or *–ed* words.

1. Watching _____ , Alex became

    very nervous about the math test.

2. Concentrating _____ , the kitten

    crouched low to the ground and prepared to attack!

3. Studying _____ , Kristina lost

    track of time and was surprised when the clock struck midnight.

Did you notice the commas that <u>follow</u> each participial phrase above? Yes, those commas are NECESSARY. Don't forget the comma when you begin a sentence with a participial phrase.

E. By the way, the words that begin participial phrases are called **participles**. Participles are –*ing* and –*ed* verb forms that act as adjectives.* They can start participial phrases or act like regular old adjectives, as below:

> the **speeding** train   a **closed** door

Below, can you fill in the blank with a participle?

The _____ bees flew over the patch of purple flowers.

*Some verbs in the past tense do not have an –ed form. See appendix for more information.

6.3 – Appositives (very ubiquitous)

(*ubiquitous* = found everywhere)

A. An appositive is a word or group of words following a noun that provides extra, unnecessary information about that noun. The heart of an appositive is a **noun** itself that renames (is another name for) the noun it follows. An appositive can be a single word or a noun plus descriptors (adjectives). An appositive may even include a descriptive prepositional phrase:

1. My son, <u>a **surfer**</u>, is six feet tall.

2. My friend accidentally crashed into the p.e. teacher, <u>a tall bearded **man**</u>, during our dodge ball game.

3. Yesterday, his boss, <u>**Mary**</u>, asked him if he could work over the weekend.

4. The train sped through Chester, <u>a small **town** near the sea</u>.

B.   **Please note that the heart of an appositive is a NOUN that is another word for the noun it follows.**

SCHOLAR ZONE

The Romans' language, Latin, is sometimes called a "dead" language because it is no longer widely spoken. The Latin that everyday Romans spoke evolved into other languages, including Spanish, Italian, French, Portuguese, and Romanian. Because of their roots in Roman Latin, these languages are called the "Romance" languages.

English has its early roots in Germanic languages, but over time many Latin words have crept into English, such as:

bona fide   per   versus

et cetera (etc.)   status quo   vice versa

Do you know the meanings of any of these Latin words and phrases?

Quick Practice #2: Below, try creating appositive phrases to describe the nouns that come just before the blank lines.

1. My school, _____ , is on East Roosevelt Street.

2. My brother gave Paul, _____ , his old guitar.

Did you notice the commas that surround each appositive above? Yes, those commas are NECESSARY. Don't forget the commas on BOTH sides of an appositive.

C. Conclusion

1. Improve your sentence variety by including participial phrases and appositives here and there.

2. Please remember that there are comma rules you **MUST** follow with appositive and participial phrases. And do you recall the comma rules we discussed regarding introductory prepositional phrases?

SCHOLAR ZONE

Slowly, English evolved, refining its Anglo-Saxon roots and absorbing words from Latin and other languages. That's how languages are: Words and phrases fall away, and new ones are added. "Internet" and "automobile" weren't words in Shakespeare's time!   Also, you wouldn't have found the word "burrito" in an English dictionary long ago, but it's part of the English language now. And what about words like "shouldst" and "thee"? So long to them—they're hardly heard anymore.

Since there was no official dictionary during the early years of the English language—the printing press would not be invented until 1450 AD—there were all sorts of spellings and all sorts of pronunciations for many English words. With the help of the printing press, spellings began to become more consistent.

Eventually, around the year 1600, the first English language dictionary was printed and published. Finally, spellings and pronunciations would become standardized. So it took about 1000 years for the foundations of the English language to be completed. **Wow... What a ride!**

Exercise 22

Part 1: Identify the underlined words as an appositive, a prepositional phrase, or a participial phrase. Write PREP, PART, or APP over the underlined words.

1. The building <u>on the corner</u> was constructed in 1883.

2. Will you please tell Mark, <u>the boy next to the window,</u> that his mom is here to pick him up?

3. <u>Typing very quickly,</u> the secretary soon finished the ten-page report.

4. <u>Exhausted from his tennis match,</u> Tom rested on the couch for the remainder of the afternoon.

5. My sister, <u>a gymnast,</u> wants to compete in the Olympics one day.

Part 2: Write sentences with various elements. Don't forget to put commas where they belong!

6. Write a sentence that <u>begins with</u> one **prepositional** phrase:

_____

_____

7. Write a sentence that includes an **appositive**:

_____

_____

8. Write a sentence that <u>begins with</u> a **participial** phrase:

_____

_____

Exercise 23

Part 1: The sentences below have participial phrases and appositives in them. Each sentence is missing ONE comma. **Add the missing comma**.

1. Opening the door a crack the burglar saw three German shepherds scampering toward him.

2. Those children, third graders painted that colorful mural in the cafeteria.

3. I am going to visit my uncle in Oregon the Beaver State.

4. Finishing second in the pie-eating contest Travis was awarded a red ribbon.

5. Completed in just six months the new bridge over the St. Johns River made it a lot easier to get to my grandmother's house.

Part 2: Take another look at the sentences above. Underline each appositive and participial phrase you see. One sentence has two participial phrases.

Part 3: Below, explain the comma rules we've covered regarding phrases.

6. A comma rule regarding prepositional phrases:

_____

_____

7. A comma rule regarding participial phrases:

_____

_____

8. A comma rule regarding appositives:

_____

_____

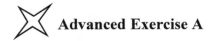 **Advanced Exercise A**

Part 1: One way to create participial phrases is to combine two sentences by turning one sentence into a participial phrase and attaching it to the front of the other sentence.

For example:

> I climbed into the back seat of the car. I had to crawl over my brother and his giant backpack.

The sentences combined:

> <u>Climbing into the back seat of the car</u>, I had to crawl over my brother and his giant backpack.

Part 2: Another way to create a sentence that has a participial phrase in it is to locate a compound sentence. Turn half of the sentence into a participial phrase and "paste" it all back together again.

For example:

> The stream glistened in the sunlight, and it gurgled as it passed over the smooth black rocks.

A new sentence that includes a participial phrase:

> <u>Glistening in the sunlight</u>, the stream gurgled as it passed over the smooth black rocks.

Do you see how combining sentences with participial phrases creates a new way of seeing for the reader? In the original sentences in both examples above, the reader sees one thing and then shifts to the next thing. In the new sentences that begin with participial phrases, the reader now holds one image in his mind and then also pulls in something additional to, in a way, see/experience two things simultaneously, which is closer to the real way people experience the world.

Activity: Skim through a piece of your own writing and see if you can find two sentences that can be combined by using a participial phrase. Write your old and new sentences down on a piece of lined paper, and then share what you've done with someone nearby. What do you think of the change?

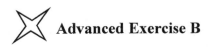 **Advanced Exercise B**

Part 1: Open up a novel and try to find one appositive and one participial phrase. For participial phrases, look for a sentence that <u>begins</u> with a participial phrase. HINT: Look in sections of the novel where there are long paragraphs and not a lot of dialogue…

Write out the sentence that has an appositive:

_____

_____

_____

_____

Write out the sentence that begins with a participial phrase:

_____

_____

_____

_____

Part 2: Find a partner to share your sentences with. **When you first sit with your partner, tell him or her about your book.** Then share the sentences you found.

What is your partner's book about?

_____

_____

_____

Did he/she do a good job finding the sentences in Part 1? (Circle one.)

      YES, DEFINITELY   MY PARTNER HAD SOME TROUBLE

APPENDIX

(Are you looking for an **answer key**? Teacher materials [answer book + evaluations] are available at middleschoolgrammar.com.)

A word about the prepositions *after*, *before*, and *until*

Students may become confused at times when dealing with words that appear on their prepositions list that can also be other parts of speech. The preposition *for* is one example of a word that often is a preposition but also can be a conjunction:

The book was <u>for my uncle</u>. (*for* is a preposition)

I woke up extra early, for I did not want to miss the bus on the first day of school. (*For* is a conjunction—a word that, along with a comma, connects two independent clauses to create one compound sentence.)

For is not a big issue since it's mostly used as a preposition and not so much as a conjunction.

The most problematic prepositions that students will encounter are *after* and *before*. These often-used words can also be subordinating conjunctions. When used as subordinating conjunctions, *after* and *before* begin groups of words <u>that also include subjects and verbs</u>. *Until* operates similarly but is less often used by middle school students.

We grabbed a snack <u>before dinner</u>. (*Before* is a preposition.)

I carefully packed my backpack <u>before I left school yesterday</u>. (*Before* is a subordinating conjunction.)

<u>After swim practice</u> we were completely exhausted. (*After* is a preposition.)

<u>After the game ended</u>, fans quickly headed to the stadium's exits. (*After* is a subordinating conjunction.)

The main thing to keep in mind is that prepositional phrases never include verbs.*   If a student creates or marks something that he or she believes to be a prepositional phrase, but something that includes a verb, they may very well be looking at a subordinate clause. Students do this a LOT when making up prepositional phrases that begin with *after* and *before*!

---

*There actually are verb forms in prepositional phrases *sometimes* with more advanced sentence structures. See appendix entry for p. 57 for a discussion of these unique verb forms. Info on p. 118 is most relevant.

Page 27

Who and *whom* are actually officially classified as both **interrogative pronouns** (when they begin questions) and **relative pronouns** (when they begin subordinate clauses).

A complete list of the personal pronouns would include the **possessive case personal pronouns**, in addition to the **objective** and **nominative cases**.

POSSESSIVE CASE PERSONAL PRONOUNS *my, mine* *your, yours* *his* *her, hers* *its* *our* *ours* *their, theirs*	NOTES While technically pronouns, these words are typically classified as <u>adjectives</u> (including predicate adjectives) when parsing sentences as they answer the adjective question "which one?" about nouns and pronouns. Also notice that *her* appears on this list as well as on the objective case personal pronoun list. In the practice exercises in this book, students trying to use *her* as a pronoun (objective case personal pronoun) often accidentally use *her* as an adjective (possessive case personal pronoun).

Page 57

As mentioned on p. 57 the word *being* is often used as a helping verb even though it does not appear in the helping verbs list at the top of the page. Here are some sentences where *being* is functioning as a helping verb:

The stamp <u>is being applied</u> to the letter by my sister.

At the gate a suspicious suitcase <u>was being searched</u> by security officers.

However, *being* and other verbs ending in *-ing* can also be classified as participles or gerunds. Participles and gerunds, like infinitives (to + verb, see p. 53), are verb forms that behave differently than traditional verbs.

<u>Participles are verbs ending in *-ing* or *-ed* that actually behave like **adjectives**</u>. (More on gerunds later.)

For example:

That crystal <u>serving </u>dish is used only for special holiday meals.

In the sentence above, *serving* describes *dish*, and therefore is a type of adjective called a **participle**. Participles are verb forms behaving like <u>adjectives</u>. *Serving* is a form of the verb "to serve" and it is something one can do, but in this sentence it's functioning as an adjective. The verb in this sentence is "is used."

Another example:

> For my birthday I had a triple-decker <u>frosted</u> cake.

In the sentence above, *frosted* describes *cake* and therefore is another example of a verb form acting like an adjective. *Frosted* <u>can</u> be a verb, as in "I frosted the cake," but in the sentence above *frosted* is serving as an adjective. The verb of the sentence is *had*.

Once again, <u>participles</u> are verbs ending in *-ing* or *-ed* that behave like <u>adjectives</u>.

Participles also may begin <u>groups</u> of words that are called **participial phrases**.

For example:

> A man <u>staring from the train's window</u> waved at me.

In the sentence above, "staring from the train's window" is what we would call a participial phrase, a group of words that begins with a participle (*staring*) and that, all together, describes a noun (*man*).

It's important for teachers to be aware of participles because <u>students will occasionally create sentences using a participle and wrongly identify the participle as the verb</u>.

For instance:

> The little kitten <u>sleeping on the windowsill</u> is so cute!

Above, *is* is the verb. "Sleeping in the windowsill" is a descriptive (adjective) phrase we would call a participial phrase.

Younger middle school students rarely use participial phrases, and so this is not a big issue, just one that a teacher should be aware of.

Previously we mentioned infinitives, which also do not behave like traditional verbs. While participles act like adjectives, infinitives are a bit more sophisticated, acting like adjectives, nouns, as well as adverbs!

Examples:

> In his <u>isolated</u> cabin in the Rocky Mountains my dad loves <u>to paint</u>.

Above, *isolated* is a participle (describing the cabin) and "to paint" is an infinitive. This infinitive is acting as a noun, for it is the <u>thing</u> the dad loves to do. The verb of this sentence is *loves*.

The driver of the <u>speeding</u> car swerved <u>to avoid the telephone pole</u>.

Above, *speeding* is a participle (describing the car) and "to avoid the telephone pole" is an infinitive phrase. This infinitive phrase is acting as an adverb. The verb of the sentence is *swerved*, and the infinitive phrase describes <u>why</u> the car swerved.

Standing in line for movie tickets, I began to chat with a nice lady wearing a fur coat.

Above, "standing in line for movie tickets" is a **participial phrase** (describing *I*) and "to chat with a nice lady wearing a fur coat" is an **infinitive phrase** acting as a noun, for it is the <u>thing</u> the person began to do. Additionally, *inside* the infinitive phrase is a participial phrase! "Wearing a fur coat" describes the lady. The verb in this sentence is *began*.

Can you imagine a student looking at the sentence above and identifying the verb as "began to chat"? It happens.

Here's a very common mistake students make when directed to compose a sentence that includes a verb phrases:

This jacket seems to be a little too big for me.

Students will consider "seems to be" a verb phrase. Actually, though, "to be a little too big for me" is an infinitive phrase, and the verb for this sentence is the single-word verb *seems*. And, by the way, *seems* (and all of its forms) is **never** a helping verb.

Of course, it has already been mentioned that infinitives are never part of THE verb in a sentences, so technically students should not be including something like "to be" in their verb anyway. However, it does happen.

To come full circle in this very long (but important!) discussion, consider the following sentence:

Joe did not like <u>being the shortest boy in his class</u>.

Above, "did like being" is something a student might consider to be the verb. It's not, though; the verb is "did like."

So what is "being the shortest boy in his class"? It certainly <u>looks</u> like a participial phrase, doesn't it?

If you think about it, though, "being the shortest boy in his class" is the THING Joe does not like, and therefore it is…a <u>noun</u> phrase! Such phrases, ones that begin with an *-ing* verb and operate as nouns, are called **gerund phrases**.

Here's a sentence with a single-word **gerund** in it:

<u>Swimming</u> is a great way to cool off in the summertime.

Swimming is the subject of this sentence. No one is doing any swimming and *swimming* is certainly not behaving like a participle here—it's a thing, an activity. Therefore, *swimming* is a gerund.

(Did you notice the infinitive phrase in the sentence?)*

Gerunds and gerund phrases, as well as infinitives and infinitive phrases, may show up in prepositional phrases from time to time, something to watch out for.

Here are some examples:

after eating lunch

(above, the object of the preposition [o.p.] is the gerund phrase "eating lunch")

without stopping

(above, the o.p. is the gerund *stopping*)

about to buy a watch

(above, the o.p. is the infinitive phrase "to buy a watch")

before pushing the button

(above, the o.p. is the gerund phrase "pushing the button")

And so <u>technically</u> it is possible to have a verb inside of a prepositional phrase! Of course, the verb does not behave like a true verb in these circumstances… This is an exception that needs no explanation up front, but it is nice for a teacher to know since students will, from time to time, create such things.

*The infinitive phrase is "to cool off in the summertime."

In conclusion, there are three verb forms that do not behave like verbs:

1. Participles are verb forms ending in either *-ing* or *-ed* that behave like adjectives.
2. Infinitives are "to + a verb" forms that behave like adjectives, nouns, or adverbs.
3. And gerunds are verb forms ending in *-ing* that behave like nouns.

As we have seen in the many examples above, participles, infinitives, and gerunds may be alone or they may begin phrases.

One more factoid: Collectively, participles, infinitives, and gerunds are sometimes called **verbals**. Phew!

Page 71

The verb "to become" is an action verb when it is used to mean *attractive*, as in "That dress is very becoming on you." This definition of the verb "to become" is very infrequently used today.

Page 105

Some verbs in English do not have past tense forms that end with *–ed*. For instance, the verb "to choose" has an irregular past tense form: *chose*. Such verbs still have past tense forms that can be used as adjectives (participles), however.

Below are some examples of verbs with irregular past participle forms:

the <u>chosen</u> students   the <u>frozen</u> broccoli   the <u>lost</u> puppy

the <u>bent</u> nail   the <u>hidden</u> treasure

Each underlined word above is a past tense form of a verb acting as an adjective, and, therefore, each is a participle (past participle).

By the way, each of the verbs above has a regular present participle form: *choosing, freezing, losing, bending,* and *hiding*.

40 Prepositions in Verse Learn the <u>prepositions</u> in context by memorizing this story!
(Gray words are repeated prepositions.)

Verse 1	Verse 2	Verse 3
<u>**About**</u> **the Old Spooky House** <u>**By**</u> **My Home**	<u>**During**</u> **My Hike and** <u>**After**</u> **My Ascent**	<u>**Inside**</u> **the Chamber** <u>**Without**</u> **a Light**
I walked <u>Into</u> the old spooky house <u>Across</u> the street, and <u>Behind</u> me The heavy door slammed shut! <u>Above</u> me A single light bulb flickered; <u>Below</u> me The floorboards creaked. <u>To</u> my left, A black umbrella hung <u>From</u> an elephant's ivory tusk. <u>To</u> my right, <u>On</u> the floor Lay an orange tiger's skin. I walked <u>Toward</u> the staircase, <u>Around</u> a large green vase, <u>Between</u> two fat white columns, And <u>up</u> the stairs I went.	<u>Along</u> the railing I slid my hand, and <u>Under</u> my feet I felt bugs crunch <u>Through</u> the window The moonlight shone <u>Over</u> the landing <u>In</u> a soft white beam. <u>At</u> the top <u>Of</u> the stairs, <u>In front of</u> me Stood a female ghost; <u>Beside</u> her Was a chestnut horse Whose tail swatted flies <u>Against</u> the wall. I said, "Hello," but <u>Instead of</u> talking, They started walking. <u>With</u> a tall white candle <u>In</u> the woman's wrinkled hand, <u>Down</u> the long, dark hall We went.	<u>Before</u> an open door We paused; <u>Near</u> me I could feel The ghost woman's breath. <u>On</u> a bed <u>Beyond</u> us Something was rustling <u>Beneath</u> purple sheets. Lightning suddenly struck <u>Next to</u> a giant oak tree, And it lit the room <u>For</u> a moment. <u>Out</u> the window Jumped the horse! <u>Off</u> the nightstand Crashed the lamp! And that's when I saw the skull <u>On</u> a pillow And rats wriggling <u>Around</u> the white bones… <u>Until</u> then, I'd never known What had become <u>Of</u> Mr. Jones!

Afterward
About Richbaub's Grammar

The foundational beliefs behind the development of the *Richbaub's* grammar materials are:

1. Grammar instruction is an important part of a writing curriculum.

2. A grammar strand must be a proper, manageable, and appropriate size.

3. Quality grammar instruction requires some "decontextualized" lessons and practice, yet a grammar program should constantly remind and show students how an awareness of grammatical concepts can be applied to improving one's speaking and writing, most specifically one's <u>academic</u> speaking and writing.

*   *   *

When teaching good comma usage, it is far easier when students can identify introductory elements like prepositional phrases, subordinate clauses, and verbal phrases. Understanding the parts of a sentence comes in handy when punctuating compound sentences or when discussing fragments and run-on sentences. In addition, teaching agreement, pronoun usage, or even, say, the difference between *well* and *good* are simplified if students have a solid foundation of grammatical knowledge and, therefore, share with their teacher a common grammatical vocabulary.

Most importantly, however, I appreciate grammar's usefulness in communicating with students about writing style. During revision, I encourage students to see how often they've begun sentences with prepositional phrases and to strive for variety in sentence beginnings by adding in an introductory adverb, subordinate clause, participle, or participial phrase. Perhaps they can move a subject <u>after</u> the verb in a sentence. I explain fragments by stating that a sentence must be a complete thought <u>and</u> have a subject and a verb. I explain weak verb choice by telling students to be aware of not depending too much on linking verbs. I ask students to remove unnecessary helping verbs. In the pursuit of longer sentences, sentence combining through the use of subordinate clauses and verbal (participial, gerund, and infinitive) phrases can be easily articulated. **It's just much easier to guide students to analyze, experiment with, and improve their own writing styles when they have a good foundation in grammar.**

During the revision process, GU&M knowledge helps one to correctly insert or delete commas, to evaluate verb usage, to vary sentence patterns, etc., all of those finer things that lead to a clean, polished, and impressive final draft.

In addition, I like what the National Council for Teachers of English (NCTE) had to say about the question "Why Is Grammar Important?":

> "Grammar is important because it is the language that makes it possible for us to talk about language. Grammar names the types of words and word groups that make up sentences not only in English but in any language…

> "People associate grammar with errors and correctness. But *knowing about* grammar also helps us understand what makes sentences and paragraphs clear and interesting and precise. Grammar can be part of literature discussions, when we and our students closely read the sentences in poetry and stories. And *knowing about* grammar means finding out that all languages and all dialects follow grammatical patterns." *(source: NCTE's Assembly for the Teaching of English Grammar, 2002)*

Simply put, spending the time to give students a substantial foundation in grammar is essential if you're planning to lead students to be as proficient in the English language as they can be. Ignoring a formal instruction of grammar during the middle school years is a mistake!

But Don't Kids Need to *Write* to Become Better Writers, Rather Than Sit Through Grammar Lessons?

Actually, the research tells us that the number one thing a person can do to become a better writer is to read! This struck me as counterintuitive at first, but it makes a lot of sense when you think about it this way: We learn by taking things in. Sitting down and writing is not taking things in; writing is output, not input.

Steven Krashen champions this idea in a small part of his book *The Power of Reading: Insights from the Research* (second edition, 2004). Citing numerous studies, Krashen summarizes:

> "More writing does not necessarily lead to better writing. Although some studies show that good writers do more writing than poor writers, increasing the amount of writing students do does not increase their writing proficiency" (135).

Reading, on the other hand, is so important to the process of becoming a better writer because through the process of reading, one is constantly fed good grammar, good writing, and interesting techniques and styles.

Writing has a higher purpose: Writing helps us think through things, or, as Krashen puts it: "Writing can help us solve problems and make us smarter" (132). Writing is thinking, and so writing is invaluable in the pursuit of knowledge and therefore invaluable to anyone who wants to become a better thinker.

There recently was a lot of hubbub about "writing across the curriculum," and this was a terrific idea, but not, as was suggested (and commonly believed), because more writing would improve students' writing skills. Rather, writing in math class would help students better think through math problems. Writing in science would help students increase the quality of their thinking about science topics, etc. In other words, the activity of writing would improve students' thinking, not necessarily their writing.

With the reading and writing workshop movement afoot, many students are doing a whole lot of writing, squeezing out time for "inputting" things like GU&M and vocabulary, which are taught only in tiny bits and pieces through "mini lessons."

The reason for all of the writing is based on a false analogy that goes like this: Practicing something makes you better at that something. For instance, when you practice playing tennis you become a better tennis player. Therefore, it certainly must follow that practicing writing will make you a better writer.

There actually is research that concludes that doing more reading will make you a better reader. As summarized by Krashen, research has shown that kids who read a lot over the summer make greater gains in their reading ability than students who do little or no reading over the summer, that students who read the most in their free time make the most gains in reading achievement, etc. etc. etc. (8-9).

The research about improving one's writing, however, is quite different. Again citing numerous studies, Krashen makes it plain: "We do not learn to write by writing… Language acquisition comes from input, not output, from comprehension, not production" (133, 136).

For developing writers, writing certainly allows students to <u>practice</u> what they have learned about good writing, but, again, writing in and of itself does not improve one's writing.

Sometimes I hear teachers encouraged to work to increase their students' "writing stamina" by having them write for longer and longer time periods, but that philosophy 1.) ignores the research about how to improve one's writing and 2.) consumes learning time that would more wisely be spent presenting information about writing for the students to take <u>in</u>.

Especially for developing writers, in addition to reading, studying the language in depth (i.e. learning new words, studying the language's grammar, usage, and mechanics), studying writing exemplars, and studying writing techniques and styles are all more important than constant writing practice!

Now, what gets ugly about the "grammar wars" is that even if you think teaching grammar is important, and most everyone does, not many people agree on how best to feed this knowledge to our students, so let me just say that the GU&M instruction that students receive through *Richbaub's* is <u>unique</u>!

Richbaub's grammar content is not over simplified, nor is it overstuffed. Most importantly, *Richbaub's* has a constant ear to how the application of grammatical concepts relates to improving one's writing, and the practice exercises you will find in *Richbaub's*—which often involve sentence composition—are not divorced from writing. Finally, the topics covered within the *Richbaub's* grammar materials have been selected because of their practicality for developing writers at the middle school level as well as for their foundational significance to higher-level GU&M concepts to which students will soon be exposed.

This special knowledge about the language does not <u>control</u> writing skill, and so it's certainly true that skill with grammar does not necessarily equate to writing skill. But an understanding of grammar must be in place if we are to give our students a chance to become *expert* writers.

It's important to consider that there's only so much GU&M a student and a curriculum should be asked to absorb—for both practical and developmental reasons. Yes, we still do want to keep actual writing activities at the forefront of writing instruction, which means that a grammar program must be of the appropriate scale. A grammar program cannot, for instance, be so large that it chokes out time for a sufficient amount of reading and writing!

But have you ever noticed how difficult it is to find a GU&M program that seems to have seriously considered both the developmental level of students and the fact that there are other things to teach besides GU&M? This puzzling situation certainly was another major force behind the creation of the *Richbaub's* grammar materials.

Taking a Long View

The development of *Richbaub's*, which includes topics in usage and mechanics as well, was a process that began not only with the practical realizations mentioned above, but also by taking aim at where students, as writers, have the potential to be at the end of their middle school years.

For instance, in the writing of the most-driven and most-talented 15-year olds, it is evident that they are able to consciously tap into their GU&M knowledge to improve their writing styles as well as to meet the technical requirements of academic writing. They understand what a subordinate clause is, and they can begin a thesis statement with one if you ask them to—and they know to follow the clause with a comma! When you write "comma splice" in the margin, these students know what you mean. They can recognize problems with parallel structure, too. Their writing has a mix of complex and simple sentences, and they work to sometimes begin with a participial phrase. In addition, they are cognizant of pronoun case usage rules, the rules of agreement, and how modifiers can be misplaced. These students also recognize active voice writing and will work to limit their use of helping and linking verbs.

Certainly, I'm not talking about mastery here; it's probably impossible to become an expert writer in one's teens! What I am talking about is what 15-year olds (8th-9th graders) are capable of, developmentally speaking, when it comes to turning GU&M knowledge into a useful tool to improve their writing (and speaking, too!)

And so when you consider what 15-year olds are capable of doing when it comes to engaging GU&M knowledge to improve the way they communicate, you wonder about what kind of foundational knowledge they should be fed in the years preceding. i.e. When a ninth-grade teacher sets out to discuss verbal phrases or sentence types—or any other advanced grammar concept students are now developmentally ready to handle—what prior knowledge should already be in place?

The Quandary of the Farsighted Middle School English/Language Arts Teacher

When communicating about writing, high school teachers frequently use grammatical terms with their students, terms like fragment, subordinate clause, misplaced modifier, preposition, conjunction, pronoun usage, run on, etc. A true understanding of such things requires a background in grammar.

Middle school is the most obvious place to deliver this background information, but there are some very big problems middle school teachers face:

1.) Traditional middle school grammar programs are gargantuan, and thus they consume way too much teaching time.

2.) Paring down a large grammar program to better fit into today's heavy reading and writing-focused curricula is a very complicated thing (ask anyone who's tried), and it's virtually impossible for an experienced, strong-minded English department to do so collectively.

3.) Current trends, therefore, favor teaching grammar with only intermittent grammar mini-lessons. A mini lesson here and a mini lesson there is a rather haphazard way to build a foundation in anything to support more advanced learning in the years ahead. The mini lesson approach for teaching grammar, more often than not, also leaves teachers scrambling to create their own lessons and lesson materials, especially if a teacher is interested in any kind of sustained teaching of important grammar concepts throughout a school year.

Good news: *Richbaub's* has been created to solve these problems for middle school English and language arts teachers!

Developing a Quality Middle School Grammar Program

Once the importance of the study of GU&M has been acknowledged and the end-of-middle-school goals have been established regarding how GU&M instruction should begin to manifest itself in students' writing, teachers of rising middle school students must decide how to approach GU&M. How much time can teachers allot to GU&M in light of the fact that they are also charged with not only studying other aspects of writing, as well as literature and vocabulary, but also (in many schools) with carving out time for students to read independently? Which GU&M topics should be covered and in what sequence? Which topics do not require formal study? Which topics should be left for future study?

Richbaub's, building on the basic grammar taught at the elementary level, completes students' foundation in rudimentary grammar. The parts of speech are reviewed, sentence parts are learned, problematic topics in mechanics are covered, and then this knowledge is applied toward developing an understanding of proper usage and improved writing style.

In addition, *Richbaub's* very clearly communicates to students that the study of grammar is all about writing, i.e. understanding the English language's patterns and components and practicing putting words together in the clearest and most effective way. Throughout *Richbaub's*, students compose sentences employing various structures and grammatical components, and improving one's writing is the specific focus of several sections of the program.

Ultimately, *Richbaub's* job is to provide a foundation in grammar for middle school writers—a foundation of "formal training" upon which students can stand and stretch upward toward their fullest potentials as writers in the months and years ahead!

After *Richbaub's Grammar*

Post-*Richbaub's*, students will have a foundation in grammar that will help them meet any challenge dealing with the nuts and bolts of the English language. For teachers, *Richbaub's* secures a context for all future references to and lessons in grammatical things, whether they are additional topics selected from a traditional GU&M text, to more immersive activities like sentence combining, to lessons in grammar woven into writing workshop activities, to even an as-needed, remedial approach to teaching GU&M.

Conclusion

Teachers often want to jump past such things as teaching the parts of speech or parsing action and linking verbs. How old fashioned! How dull! But try to explain fragments to high school students by discussing subjects and verbs, and you'll only get a sea of blank faces! Get into a discussion about good verb usage, and, um, what's that, Tommy? "What's a *linking* verb?" How do you begin to explain such a thing to students to whom no one's ever taken the time to teach grammar? And exactly how does one teach students the difference between *me* and *I* without mentioning prepositional phrases, subjects, or complements? Etc., etc., etc.

My point is that if you want your students to <u>really</u> understand the language, you must lay the groundwork, and that means taking the time to teach some grammar.

Unfortunately, well-meaning teachers find it difficult to properly scale a grammar strand to fit into their curriculum… And so they give up. It is nearly <u>impossible</u> to find a manageable or sensible way to trim down the content of textbooks focused on grammar.

But that's exactly what *Richbaub's* is designed to do!

Once again, *Richbaub's* provides a foundation in grammar for middle school writers—a foundation of "formal training" upon which students can stand and stretch up toward their fullest potentials as writers in the months and years ahead!

No matter where your students are headed after *Richbaub's*, you can be sure that they have received content that is suitable in scale, rich in content, and appropriate to their developmental level.

And for teachers, *Richbaub's* is the grammar strand you've been looking for as it fits seamlessly beside the literature, writing, and vocabulary study in today's middle school English classrooms.

Welcome to *Richbaub's*!

Rich Gieson

NOTES

NOTES

CPSIA information can be obtained
at www.ICGtesting.com
Printed in the USA
LVHW012148040820
662391LV00009B/572

9 781724 727572